Body Beats to Build On

A Fiction Writer's Resource

Plus Journal

April W Gardner

Body Beats to Build On:
A Fiction Writer's Resource Plus Journal
©2019 by April W Gardner

Cover design: Carpe Librum Book Designs
Big Spring Press logo: Karen Gardner

All rights reserved. No part of this book may be reproduced or transmitted in any form or by any means, electronic or mechanical, including photocopying, recording, or by an information storage and retrieval system—except by a reviewer who may quote brief passages in a review to be printed in a magazine, newspaper, or on the Web—without permission in writing from the publisher.

Library of Congress Control Number: 2019915001
ISBN-13: 978-1-945831-19-5

Published by Big Spring Press
San Antonio, Texas

Printed in the United States of America.

Table of Contents

Table of Contents	3
Introduction	10
Chapter One: Body Movement	13
Foreward Motion	13
Slow Pace	13
Moderate Pace	14
Jogging Pace	15
Running Pace	16
Legs In Motion	17
Backward Motion	18
Stopping	19
Turning	20
Rising	21
Sitting	21
Squatting	23
Leaning	23
Chapter Two: Frame and Posture	25
Shoulders	25
Shrugging	25
Slumping	26
Squaring	27
Backbone	27
Stiffening	27
Relaxing	29
Shivers And Unsteadiness	29
Muscle And Sinew	31
Chapter Three: Skin	33
Goosebumps	33
Blushing	34
Pallor	37
Sweat	38
Chapter Four: Appendages	40

Legs	40
Weakening And Buckling	40
Bending And Firming	41
Knees	42
Positions	42
Weakening	43
Firming	43
Arms	44
Crossed	44
Embracing	45
Hands And Fingers	46
Making A Fist	46
Fists Or Hands On Hips	47
Pointing	47
Miscellaneous	47
Chapter Five: Breathing	49
Holding And Losing Breath	49
Shaking Breath	51
Inhaling And Gasping	52
Exhaling	54
Active Breathing	57
Chapter Six: Internal Systems	60
Heart, Chest, And Ribs	60
Constricting Or Freezing	60
Rejoicing	61
Skipping Or Stuttering	61
Speeding	62
Dropping Or Vacating	64
Hurting	65
Chest	65
Pulse, Veins, Blood	66
Slowing And Stopping	66
Faltering	67
Surging	67
Pounding	68

Stomach And Center	69
Burning Or Freezing	69
Coiling, Clenching, Or Knotting	70
Sinking	71
Rebelling	71
Positive Emotion	72
Negative Emotion	73
Flexible Emotion Beats	74
Chapter Seven: Head	75
Motions	75
Shaking	75
Nodding	75
Rearing Back	76
Turning Neck	76
Tipping Sideways	77
Facial Expressions	77
Flexible Emotion Beats	77
Eyebrows And Forehead	80
Chapter Eight: Eyes	84
Basic Actions	84
Unfocused	84
Narrowing	85
Widening	86
Closing And Opening	87
Side Eye	88
Emotion In The Eyes	88
Positive Emotion	88
Negative Emotion	89
Flexible Emotion Beats	91
Looking To Or Away	93
Looking To	93
Looking Away	96
Locking On	96
Seeking	98
Examining	98

Lashes And Blinking	99
Tears	100
Chapter Nine: Nose And Ears	104
Nose	104
Nostrils Widening	104
Miscellaneous Beats	104
Smell	105
Ears And Hearing	107
Chapter Ten: Mouth, Teeth, And Tongue	108
Mouth	108
Bunched Mouth	108
Flat Mouth	108
Miscellaneous Beats	109
Teeth	109
Tongue	111
Wet/Dry	111
Speaking Tongue	112
Unspeaking Tongue	113
Miscellaneous Beats	115
Chapter Eleven: Smiles	117
Smiling Verbs	117
Smirks	123
Half Smiles	125
Fake And Contained Smiles	126
Full Smiles	127
Chapter Twelve: Laughter And Frowns	129
Laughter	129
Sound Qualities	129
Quiet	130
Loud	131
Unexpected	133
Freed	134
Restrained Or Forced	135
Failed	136
Negative Laughter	136

- Frowns — 137
  - Dissolving Smiles — 137
  - Sad Frowns — 138
  - Angry Frowns — 140

Chapter Thirteen: Jaw, Chin, And Throat — 141
- Jaw — 141
  - Hardening — 141
  - Circling And Jutting — 142
  - Sagging — 142
- Chin — 143
  - Up — 143
  - Down — 144
- Throat And Swallowing — 145
  - Tightening — 145
  - Swallowing — 145
  - Dryness In Throat — 147
  - Acid In Throat — 147
  - Thickening Or Aching — 148

Chapter Fourteen: — 151

- Non-Facial Emotion Beats — 151
  - Experiencing Emotion — 151
  - Containing Or Falsifying Emotion — 156

Chapter Fifteen: Thesaurus — 157
- Expressions, Gazes, Smiles — 157
- Smiles And Laughter Only — 164
- Expressions And Gazes Only — 167
- Smiles Only — 170
- Laughter Only — 171

Bonus Material: Dialogue Tags — 173
- Anger/Clipped Speech — 174
- Happiness/Laughing — 175
- Sadness/Crying — 176
- Fear/Broken Speech — 176
- Stating/Explaining — 177

Replying	177
Questioning/Wondering	177
Adding/Interrupting	178
Continuing/Repeating	178
Proclaiming/Promising	178
Agreeing	178
Deceiving/Evasion	179
Guessing/Using Caution	179
Suggesting/Using Discretion	179
Pushing One's Opinion	179
Deciding/Reassuring	179
Surprise	180
Bragging	180
Remembering	180
Revealing	180
Consoling	180
Stopping/Starting	181
Growling/Grumbling	181
Voice Raised	181
Voice Lowered	182
Whisper Beats	182

To Grace, my #1 fan.

---

body beat (noun) \ ˈbä-dē \ ˈbēt

1. : in a work of fiction, any action that brings about motion in the human body whether internal or external
//Tom's *heart pounded*.
//Sally *squared her shoulders*.

2. : the manner or method in which a character uses their physical body to express emotion
//At the sight of her, Harry's *jaw unhinged*.

Introduction

As the title implies, *Body Beast to Build on, a Fiction Writer's Resource Plus Journal* isn't intended as an instructional craft book but as a ready source of inspiration for building those million-and-one body beats found in every work of fiction. Even so, a basic understanding of body beats will go a long way toward stretching this book's value.

The terms "action beat" and "body beat" are sometimes mistakenly used interchangeably. The truth is, body beats *are* action beats, but not all action beats are body beats.

In fiction, action takes place on several levels, from broad to narrow. Broad action beats are any mass movement occurring on the page and often span a paragraph or more. They are seen through a wide lens, can be caused by people or objects, and reveal little to no detail. Think, a sports stadium as seen from a blimp's POV—cars parking in the massive lots, people streaming into the building, seats filling with team colors.

As action beats narrow, the lens tightens, and the details become clearer—a soccer ball as seen by a spectator skids across a grassy field, spinning and curving toward the kicker's teammate. When the teammate's cleat stamps down on the ball to stop its flight, we've zoomed the lens to an even narrower setting and have arrived at body beats. We could go tighter by keying in on the sting of the ball as it smacks against the player's foot, on the adrenaline spiking his pulse, or on the burn of sweat dripping into his eyes.

It's that finely honed level of action at which emotion is conveyed by the author and felt and *lived* by the reader.

Without body beats, fiction risks dullness and reduces its potential to grab a reader's emotional loyalty.

Body beats are close-up encounters with the character. Other qualifiers: they are limited to the body (unless the body is influencing an object) and are generally no more than a phrase or single sentence.

Examples of body beats include climbing a ladder, blinking back tears, swinging a tennis racket, beating down the chest-scorching rise of anger, and any other infinite number of actions that involve the body. In this book, however, we don't care about the *infinite*, only about those that repeat frequently, such as walking, breathing, and gazing. Those are the most irksome to use since we must write them again and again while avoiding repetition, a process that can stall and frustrate story creation as well as that elusive muse.

Hence, the purpose of this book—to allow a writer to choose a specific beat, skim available options, and swiftly plug in a sigh constructed differently from previous instances.

I've organized the material according to body part or function. Apart from a few (hey, there are only so many ways to say "hands on hips"), each motion includes enough options to give your beats diversity, make your writing shine, and keep readers on their toes. That said, my lists are far from complete. Body beats, even the repetitious ones, can be arranged in oodles of ways, which is why the print edition includes journaling columns to record any others you that occur to you.

The blanks found in certain beats can be filled any way you'd like (see THESAURUS, pg. 157) but will benefit most from words conveying emotion. For example, "___ sent a blip/glitch/hiccup to his heartbeat" (page 61) can become "excitement sent a hiccup to his heartbeat" or "her heartbeat hiccupped with fear" or "her touch sent a glitch to his heart."

To allow your imagination room to build on, I've distilled most of the beats to bare bones. Others are written in almost complete sentences, having been taken from my own works. Feel free to copy and paste the beats exactly as provided or use them simply as a launching pad for inspiration.

Let your imagination loose and be creative. Most importantly, get that manuscript written!

April W Gardner

Chapter One: Body Movement

—FOREWARD MOTION—

→ Substitutes for *footsteps*: footfalls, footpads, gait, paces, steps, strides, tracks, tread

Slow Pace
- ambled over
- clumped along
- dragged along
- drew up to
- drifted near
- meandered in
- minced steps/forward
- nipped sideways
- picked his way toward
- schlepped along
- sidled up
- slogged her way
- slunk forward
- stodged along
- stole to
- took a few faltering steps
- trudged after him
- trundled past
- ushered a few steps
- crept forward
- feet went into motion/action

Moderate Pace
- ___ carried her toward
- ___ marked her every step
- ___ strides brought her to
- a clipped pace/clipped out of the room
- advanced on her
- aimed her steps at
- approached at a tramping/slinking pace
- beckoned her forward
- betook herself to
- carried herself off
- crossed to
- finished the distance
- footed into the room
- footsteps carried her to
- furthered into the room
- galumphed away
- glided past
- halved the distance to
- his feet took him to
- in lockstep with/behind him
- issued into the hall
- made a straight line for
- moved in/up/on
- one foot overtook the other
- paced off a short distance

- prowled forward
- returned to him
- set out for
- stalked nearer
- strolled from sight
- swaggered forward
- swanned through the place
- the clop of boots sounded
- took off toward
- took to his heels
- trailed in
- traipsed through
- traversed the lawn
- tromped/tramped across
- trooped past
- trounced along
- trucked off

Jogging Pace
- danced/pranced forward
- ferried herself away
- hoofed it out of there
- jotted across the lot
- flounced/prissed out of the room
- gamboled/skipped/frolicked
- opened her stride
- tripped across the room

- marched steps carried her
- whisked herself away
- left at speed

Running Pace
- a long-legged lope
- a stamping fit
- barreled ahead
- torpedoed past
- beat feet out of there
- heels beat the ground hard
- bounded up
- broke into a jog/run/lope/trot
- clambered after him
- cut/obliterated the space between them
- double-timed it out of there
- feet swifted her along
- feet took wing
- ground passed beneath him
- haring off/rabbited away
- hoofing it
- landed heavy feet on
- pelted down the street
- plunged ahead
- powered along the path

- put on a burst of speed
- raced toward
- running full tilt
- sallied forth
- shot on unsteady legs toward
- threw himself into a sprint
- thundered toward
- tore off
- volleyed up the stairs
- went off hot foot
- zipped along

Legs in Motion
- legs propelled her along
- got his legs moving
- legs managed a bit more speed
- legs pumped/churned
- ___ gave flight to his legs
- churning legs covered the ground
- put fire in/under her feet
- legs devoured the field
- legs took off toward
- legs jolted into motion
- legs took a ___ path/trail/course
- long legs ate up the ground
- put wings to his legs
- fire coursed through his legs

- legs carried him/bore him away
- great push of his legs
- lent power to his legs
- legs scrambled into motion
- coerced/urged legs into moving/greater speed
- legs fought to keep up speed
- legs stretched farther into their stride
- willed her legs to move faster
- legged it
- legs begged her to run

> Other useful forward action words: bustle, dash, hasten, jog, scamper, scramble, scurry, scuttle, sprint

—BACKWARD MOTION—

- a back-stepped scramble
- backtracked/backpedaled
- canceled/rescinded his progress
- contra-strides
- dropped one foot back
- fell/reeled back
- fumbled in reverse
- gave ground
- inverse/contrary stride

- pulled/edged away
- rescinding/retracting steps
- retreated/retired a few steps
- reversal of steps
- scuttled off/backwards
- sent him back ___ paces
- shrank/cringed back
- skittered backwards
- surrendered/conceded/ relinquished a step

—STOPPING—

→ Substitutes for *stopped*: halted, paused, quit, stalled

- came to a fast halt
- checked his flight
- crashed to a halt
- drew up/stopped short
- halted his advance
- killed his speed
- planted/rooted his feet
- pulled up fast
- put on the brakes
- rested on his heels (paused)
- stilled/froze

—TURNING—

→ Substitutes for *turned*: rotated, swiveled, whirled

- ___ compelled/coaxed her about
- ___ pivoted him on the ball of his foot
- ___ reeled her toward
- ___ slued him around
- bent his steps toward
- faced his eyes front/back/toward
- gyrated toward
- he rounded on her/rounded back
- made a turnabout
- made an about-face
- on a reverse twist
- she flipped toward him
- shoved around on the ball of his foot
- swung/ripped around
- veered/swerved/twisted away
- wheeled/wrenched away
- whipped about/a whip-about
- whorled about

—RISING—

→ Substitutes for *rose*: got up, stood

- ___ bolted him upright
- ___ compelled/brought her up
- claimed/gained her feet
- clambered/scrambled to his feet
- fought to her feet
- he took/found his feet
- heaved himself up
- hoisted herself to her feet
- lifted herself out of the chair
- propelled herself up
- punched/shot/surged upright
- pushed himself to standing
- put her feet beneath her
- shoved upright
- sprang/jerked to standing
- uncoiled from the ground/to her feet
- unfurled to standing

—SITTING—

- claimed a chair
- dropped down next to him
- dumped himself down on

- eased his joints to the earth/chair
- ensconced/installed himself in the seat
- flopped into a chair
- grabbed a seat/seated his tired bones
- knees buckling, he sank to
- lowered herself
- melted into the recliner
- parked himself in/on
- perched on/shunted onto the stool
- pitched herself into
- placed himself on the couch
- plonked his backside onto
- plopped himself down/down on his butt
- posed prettily/menacingly on the stool
- relaxed into the chair
- sagged/slumped onto the bench
- settled in/onto
- slid into place on the
- took a place at/on
- tossed himself into the chair
- folded his frame into the seat

—SQUATTING—

- bending at the knees, she lowered
- bent knees tight and low
- cowered low
- cringed/tucked her body down into a huddle
- crouched down/groundward
- descended/sank to a crouch
- down on his haunches
- drew/bowed downward
- dropped on her heels
- flexed her knees
- hunkered/huddled/scrooched/ bunkered down
- knelt down
- sat/perched on his heels
- squatted/roosted on his hunkers
- stooped into a squat

—LEANING—

→ Substitutes for *leaned*: angled, canted, inclined, pitched, tipped, tilted, slanted, sloped

- a sigh/defeat slumped her against
- angled her body onto

- braced forearm on the doorframe
- keeled against the wall
- lounged against
- propped a shoulder against
- rested his biceps against
- shored his leaning frame on
- shoulder bore him up
- sloped her sagging body against
- supported himself with an elbow on

Chapter Two: Frame and Posture

→ Substitutes for *body*: build, bulk, figure, form, frame, length, shape, torso

—SHOULDERS—

Shrugging
- his shoulder bobbed
- shoulders jounced
- scrunched her shoulders against her neck
- hunched her shoulders up
- hefted/hoisted a shoulder
- shrug rolled over her shoulders
- a jostle of the shoulder
- rolled a thick/bony shoulder
- indifference/ambivalence bounced her shoulder
- his shoulder jolted/ flinched/lurched
- jerked shoulders in a shrug
- shrug jarred him
- shoulders twitched/ twitched a shoulder
- nudged a rueful shrug

- a bewildered/perplexed shrug
- neglectful shrug
- lifted a blasé/sulky shoulder
- little hop of her shoulders
- bumped a shrug
- shrugged internally

Slumping
- shoulders hunched forward
- slouched shoulders
- took on rounded shape of inevitability/insecurity
- dread/loss collapsed shoulders
- fell/sank into a bowed heap
- shoulders collapsed/drooped/wilted/lowered/deflated/folded/flagged/slipped/declined/sagged
- shoulders eased/gravitated earthward
- ___ sloped tension from his shoulders
- rolled-in/curving shoulders
- shoulders pointed down
- humiliation/shame crumpled her spine
- body sagged/neck shrank
- shoulders went/bent concave

Squaring
- pinned/fastened/fixed his shoulders back
- shoulders rolled back
- pushed her shoulders back
- made rigid her shoulders
- drove/flung/pitched/pushed her shoulders in place
- squeezed/pressed or clinched/barred his shoulder blades together
- the set of his shoulders/he set his shoulders
- shoulder muscles locked
- flattened/leveled/evened her shoulders
- shoulders sat low and back
- locked/squared her shoulders
- shoulders blades drew together
- spread his shoulders

—BACKBONE—

→ Substitutes for *backbone*: back, posture, ridge of her back, spinal column, spine, vertebrae

Stiffening
- backbone stretching
- stretched backbone to full length

- back became a ramrod
- backbone clicked into a rod
- posture firming
- squared posture
- deliberately uncurled/unfolded her vertebrae
- firmly aligned her backbone
- stiffened herself straight
- made her back strong/proud
- ratcheted her spine
- made plumb her backbone/ backbone plumbline straight
- ridge of her back went straight
- made backbone a rod/ shaft/dowel
- frame went arrow-/lance-straight
- his spine whipped/snapped straight
- infused his backbone with iron/steel/flint
- imbued her spine with resolve/determination
- squared her posture
- neck lengthened
- spine locked/clenched/bolted/ bowed/hunched

Relaxing
- posture bled tension
- sagging frame
- starch in her frame dissolved
- sapped the arch from her spine
- his aggressive posturing eased
- set of his frame relaxed
- relaxed her backbone
- posturing uncertain

> See SHOULDERS (page 25) for more ideas.

Shivers and Unsteadiness
- shivers nipped her spine
- quiver tripped up her back
- shivering in her skins
- rake of shivers crawled/coursed
- itching sensation scrambled up/over her
- ___ quivered through his muscles
- body all shivery
- fear skittered around his skin
- chills iced her spine
- ice crusted over her backbone
- tremors convulsed her ribs
- quiver ran down her frame

- tremors coursed her shoulders
- spine/bones wobbled
- chilled the bones
- a body-wringing/spine-dithering
- shivers traveled her length
- ___ shimmied up his bones
- deep-muscle shakes
- rattled his teeth/bones/courage
- shiver ran crookedly/ jaggedly through her body
- racking quakes
- shudder throttled her spine
- muscle-spasming shiver
- shiver cut through her/ feathered over her skin
- skated/snaked over him
- a shudder rocked her
- tremors befell her
- shudder worked through his backbone
- shudder echoed through him
- jellied his spine
- fury/shivers jostled him

> Shivers can affect the arms, backbone, body, bones, frame, shoulders, and spine.
> Shivers can jerk/wrench/yank the body.

—MUSCLE and SINEW—

→ Substitutes for *muscle*: brawn, flesh, meat, might, power, stamina, strength, tissue, vigor

- lethal/deadly/violent brawn
- popped with strain
- sinews bulged
- tightened with readiness
- hardened over bones and under skin
- felt the swell of his muscles
- muscles in his punching arm thickened/begged release
- fixity of his muscles
- spasm cinched his muscles
- ___ quivered through his muscles
- ___ constricted the muscles of his back
- firm sculpt of muscle
- carved musculature
- muscle flared in refusal
- fight swelled her muscles
- ___ taxed/strained his muscles
- stout muscles locked down
- tension in muscles surrendered/ gave way
- muscles eased a fraction

- loosened her coiled muscles
- muscles went flaccid/limp/soft
- every muscle relaxed
- taut muscles deflated/weakened
- muscles grateful for a rest/reprieve
- kinks/knots in muscles
- play/shift of muscle beneath the skin

-Sinew is often compared to cords, jute, rope, twine.
-Tired muscle quivers and twitches—see KNEES, WEAKENING (page 48) for more ideas.
-Muscles can bulge, bunch, burn, cinch, clench, coil, cord, contract, flare, flex, harden, melt, ripple, spasm, strain, swell, tick, tighten, thicken, twist, twitch.

Chapter Three: Skin

—GOOSEBUMPS—

- gooseflesh pebbled her arms
- skin became erect with bumps/ became a rash of fear
- flesh tightened/constricted against the cold
- prickle of ___ rampaged her flesh
- ___ pricked at her skin
- tingle ran down his back
- pinpricks of
- cold crabbed up her legs
- erupted in pimples
- goose-pimpled skin
- skin crawled with
- cold-prickled skin
- his skin sparked
- flesh came alive with
- tingles of ___ scaled his body
- tingles frolicked along
- ___ pulled chills up her arms
- flood of goosebumps scattered
- ___ tingled over his scalp

- goosebumps sprayed over
- peaked his skin
- skin tightened over bones
- raised ___ across her body
- tiny hairs flickered/shot to attention
- chill bumps formed
- ___ covered her skin with a chill
- skin became gooseflesh
- skin-tightening water/wind/cold
- ___ shimmied up him

-Goosebumps can replicate feathers, bugs, or spider webs on the skin.
-Skin can also bristle, pinch, ripple, and tickle.

—BLUSHING—

- heat/color touched her cheeks
- color mantled her cheeks
- cheeks flamed
- color whooshed up his neck
- a streak of heat across his skin

- a shot of color to his ___
- shame bruised her cheeks
- heat traveled in a slow wave across/up
- heat radiated from her neck/chest/face
- rage/humiliation burned up his neck
- heat diffused off her cheeks/chest
- warmth of a blush suffused
- an eruption of pink
- pink-stained skin
- cheeks pinked/pinkened
- fury/shame-pinkened cheeks
- blush bit into her cheeks
- blushed an angry/violent red
- blushed furiously/savagely/hotly
- flush rose to his cheeks
- fire crackled beneath her skin
- anger/lust seared his skin
- heightened color
- face prickled into a blush
- blush tickled up the back of her neck
- rosy hue/shade colored her throat

- fire filled/blazed across her cheeks
- chest roasted/toasted
- heat climbed her ___
- stains of ___ rose on her
- ___ mottled her skin
- blush stole over/crept up
- humiliation glowed bright on
- flaming blush assailed/assaulted
- flush of ___ on his face
- skin crackled with heat
- colored brightly
- neck went florid
- heat invaded her skin
- crimson/ruddy/florid with
- color splotched his face
- blotches of red erupted on
- his color/hue reddened/went rosy
- roseate tint to her face
- blush ambushed her
- warmth smacked/slapped his cheeks
- warmth of a blush
- heat stormed/roared up her neck
- heat-borne shame/anger flooded his chest
- ___ made heat touch her cheeks

- heat scalded her to the rims/tips of her ears
- heat bolted/leapt up from her chest
- tingle of shame
- color rode/capped/crowned her cheeks
- cheeks felt like ___ (she'd stood too near a fire, been too long in the sun, etc.)
- a flush like sunrise
- feverish flush
- splotches of color on
- cheeks hot with
- flushed fifty/a dozen shades of red
- blush died down

> Colors for blushing: apple, beet, blood, bubblegum, crimson, carmine, carnation, carnelian, cherry, cherry-blossom pink, claret, coral, dusty rose, garnet, lurid, pink, rose, ruby, ruddy, russet, scarlet, wine

—PALLOR—

- blood/color drained from
- ___ siphoned blood from
- cheeks deathly/sickly white

- color leeched from
- face paled with
- she blanched
- face went bloodless
- pale as a
- face glowed pale
- looked pale and drawn
- face washed of color

—SWEAT—

- sheen of sweat/moisture formed
- a pebble/bead/pearl of sweat trickled
- face glistened/gleamed with sweat
- a glaze of sweat broke out
- sweat coasted down his
- mist of cold sweat
- sweat decorated/painted his
- sweat-slathered/slathered brow
- sweat-covered/slicked skin
- blinked sweat from eyes
- burst from his face
- poured from him/down his body
- streamed into eyes
- clammy skin
- sweat puddled in his palms

- slicked her palms
- layer of icy sweat
- sprang from pores
- trickled a path between breasts
- trailed his hairline
- beaded at hairline/on upper lip
- licked down his jaw
- chilled his skin
- dripped off his hair
- droplets slid down
- sweat made a stink
- dried tacky on his
- dampened his pits
- glistened on the back of his neck
- shone oily on his forehead

Chapter Four: Appendages

—LEGS—

Weakening and Buckling
- turned legs to Jell-O
- legs/knees became faint
- gelatinous legs/became gelatin
- lost strength in his legs
- untried/unproven legs
- couldn't feel his legs
- numbness crept into
- legs became faint
- legs near surrender
- legs gave up/surrendered
- fatigue flooded her legs
- his spent legs
- depleted/drained legs
- legs threatened to give way
- unsound/uncertain/unsure legs
- boneless/weary legs
- feckless/untrustworthy legs
- watery legs/turned to water
- legs felt like lead/stone/anchors
- trembled/wobbled/shook/warbled/buckled/caved/yielded/folded
- legs wouldn't support her

- muscles in legs burned
- muscles twitched/cramped with fatigue
- legs protested work/exertion
- refused to function
- became pulp/pulpy

Bending and Firming

→ Substitutes for *crossed* legs: crisscrossed, folded, tucked

- legs curled beneath him
- bunched legs preparing to leap/sprint
- hardened the muscles of his legs
- firmed/powered his stance
- stiffened/strengthened/cemented/planted/rooted legs
- spread for balance/akimbo
- set firmly apart
- legs braced
- injected strength/resolve into his stance
- steadied his legs
- menacing/confident spread of his legs
- went rigid

—KNEES—

Positions
- while seated: splayed, set wide, spread
- knees to chest/drawn up/upraised/bent/folded
- cheek/forearms rested on upraised knees
- hugged her knees
- arms wrapped around knees
- arms hooked over raised knees
- hands/elbows on knees for support
- dropped face between knees
- forehead/chin to knees
- doubled over her knees
- down on knees
- hunkered down on knees
- ___ sent him to his knees
- on bended knees
- propped himself on his knees
- pulled/dragged knees beneath him
- got her knees under her
- stood on/shoved to knees

Lowering to knees: collapse, crash, crumple, drive, drop, fall, pitch, sink, slam, slump, stumble, stutter, wilt

Weakening
- knees fading strength
- knees quivering
- felt hollow/woozy
- softened knees
- went weak in the knees
- turned knees to mush
- fickle knees
- lost reliability
- rubbery knees
- water-kneed
- ___ wrecked her knees
- threatened to double/quit
- knees caved
- sapped starch from knees
- ___ sucked/siphoned command from his knees
- stopped working

Firming
- locked/braced
- snapped knees straight
- straightened knees
- girded his knees for

- tightened/steeled her knees against
- bolstered her knees to support

—ARMS—

Crossed

→ Substitutes for *crossed arms*: folded, linked, pinned, pleated, twined

- pinned her crossed arms over her chest
- settled/linked arms over her bosom
- pleated her arms across her breasts
- crossed arms broadened him/ bulged muscles
- crossed her arms in front of herself
- arms knotted/laced over her chest
- an indignant/stubborn fold of his arms

Avoid the awkward phrase "*cross*ed arms a*cross* chest."

Embracing

- gathered her in/into his arms
- the circle of his arms
- encircling arms
- pulled/drew her to him
- put/wrapped/wound her arms around him
- bundled her into his arms
- his arms twined about her
- arms locked about his neck/shoulders/waist/midriff
- stretched her body against his
- a lung-compressing clutch
- bruising lock on her
- crushing her close
- reeled her into his arms
- cradled in his arms
- a rib-punishing squeeze
- embraced herself
- held her arms around herself
- arms wrapped about herself/her own ribs
- hugged her elbows
- her hands cupped her elbows

Embraces can also be shown in the position of the bodies—hands on the lower back, her face in his neck, etc. (example beat: his palms flat against her lower back).

—HANDS and FINGERS—

Making a Fist
- clenched her hands
- fingers folded in and tightened
- nails gouged his palms
- scored nails into his palms
- dug fingernails into palms
- joints of fist burned
- fist begged to be let loose
- strained skin over curling knuckles
- fingers curled in on themselves
- knuckles burned
- fists balled hard/ball of his fist
- sledgehammer fists
- flexed his hand
- squeezed her hands into fists
- fingers coiling into tight balls
- fists tingled/yeared to strike
- knuckles coiled and bleached
- fingers hinged and unhinged/ clenched and unclenched
- hands bunched/closed into fists

Fists or Hands on Hips

→ Verbs for placing hands on hips: fisted, planted, shelved, stacked, stationed

Pointing

→ Substitutes for *pointed*: gesticulated, gestured, indicated, motioned, trained on/toward

- hitched a thumb toward
- jabbed a finger/thumb toward
- thumbing at
- tilted his chin at
- nudged her chin toward
- lifted his chin that direction
- gesturing her chin at
- used his chin to direct her to

Miscellaneous
- palms itched to
- fingernails drummed/clicked against
- angry fingers choked ___ (an object)
- waggled a finger at him
- throwing/casting up his hands
- flung his hands out
- flipped her palms up

- twisted her hands together
- picked at/chewed her fingernails
- tips of fingers at corners of eyes
- pinched the bridge of his nose

-Fingers of different hands can be absorbed by another's, bridged with another's, clasped, encased, folded, fused, knotted through another's, laced, linked, married, rounded about, wound together, or woven.

-Fingers can do the following to hair: bury, claw through, dig, drive, entwine, fish, lock on, plow, rake, sink into, spread into/through, tease through, thrust into, thread, or twine.

-Fingers can bite, brush, caress, cup, clamp, curve around, dig, finger, flutter, slide, slip, stroke, trace, trail, trap, or wrap.

Chapter Five: Breathing

→ Interchangeable terms: air, breath, chest, lungs, ribcage, ribs, wind

—HOLDING and LOSING BREATH—

- ___ stoppered her wind
- ___ congealed/clotted her air
- breath became a syrup/sludge
- ___ crowded the air from his chest
- backed up her breath
- clenched her lungs
- shock/tears occluded her breath
- ___ nearly squeezed off her air
- impaired/blunted or broken/spoiled breathing
- robbed of breath
- shackled/chained/bound up her wind
- ___ tore the breath from her lungs
- air in his lungs evaporated/vanished/faded
- struck breathless
- bated breath

- couldn't grasp air
- breath grew thin/spare
- air deserted her lungs
- breath snagged in her throat
- breath collected/collected her breath
- breath left her chest
- trapped wind in her chest
- lungs/breath held hostage
- lungs suspended
- breath-pinching fear
- bubble of air cooped/stuck in her lungs
- she stiffened/hardened/stilled her lungs
- breath solidified in chest
- her wind constricted/pinched off
- choked on her breath
- the air in her lungs expired/went stale/stagnant
- a knot/blister/lump of air caught in her chest
- his chest seized up
- lungs frozen full/at peak
- incapacitated/crippled/maimed breath

- breath cowering/cringing in her lungs
- breath recoiled to back of throat

—SHAKING BREATH—

- ___ reduced her breath to a wheeze/an erratic rasp
- breath hitched/staggered/ stumbled/stuttered
- took in a shuttering/shuddery breath
- made his breath go shallow/thin/ slight/light
- ragged breath spoke of
- breath harried in his throat
- shook with tattered breath
- inhaled a stuttery breath
- breath turned/became shaky
- sucked in stutter-breaths
- irregularity of breathing
- struggling/battling lungs
- riffling/rippling/ruffling breast
- trembling/fluttering release of breath
- breath coarsened/roughened
- breathing serrated/razored/ sawed between his teeth

—INHALING and GASPING—

→ Substitutes for *inhale*: breathe in, inbreath, inhale, inhalation, intake

- ___ swelled the lungs
- tiny, abrupt intake
- drew a thoughtful breath
- inhaling courage/patience/etc.
- visibly inhaling
- rattled/grabbed a lung-filling inhale
- air whizzed over teeth/into lungs
- gulped down a steadying breath
- drew a lungful of air/oxygen
- allowed/forced starved lungs to draw air
- breast swelled with an inbreath
- a drag/haul of air
- sucked/pulled at the air
- gulped down a steadying breath
- chest rose in pursuit/search of air
- chest puffed out with a ___ inhale
- drowned his lungs with air
- took a gulp of air

- pulled breath through nostrils
- took a cleansing breath
- tight chest labored to expand/fill up
- rapid pull of wind into lungs
- air whistled through her throat
- crisply indrawn breath
- air skidded/stuttered down his throat
- nostrils flared/burned with lungs' drag
- lungs jolted and slurped air
- need for air expanded his nostrils
- pulled air in sharply/deliberately
- quaffed the air
- lungs jerked back into action
- lungs kicked back to life in a flood
- filled lungs to capacity
- her entire being drew a breath of
- filled his scrawny/muscular frame with air

—EXHALING—

→ Substitutes for *exhale*: breathe out, exhalation, outbreath
→ Useful verbs for *exhale*: discarded, dumped, expelled, jettisoned, shed, sloughed, unloaded

- breath eased out
- took a ___ breath and sighed it out
- seepage of breath
- let out a long swoosh of air
- released a protracted/leaking/drawn-out exhale
- leaked from lungs in long/lingering stream
- air eked from her throat
- she exhaled long
- blew out his cheeks
- breath soughed from her
- breath blew thinly
- constricted/shrank/tightened his lungs in a slow leak
- released a stifled/smothered/strangled breath
- jetted air/a hiss through a crack in the lips/tight lips
- hissed out a breath
- breath rushed out on a sigh/groan/grunt/moan

- discharged a grunted breath
- ejected an open-mouthed/tight-lipped huff
- lungs flattened/deflated
- lungs emptied hard/fast
- drove out a harsh sigh
- a pained/relieved breath passed his teeth
- sighed explosively
- he sigh-growled
- breathed out briskly through her teeth
- air fled/escaped her flared nostrils
- blew/puffed air through distended nostrils
- air left his nostrils in a rush
- chuffed aggravation through an open mouth
- breath shuttled out/through
- heavy/hefty/weighty/stout exhale
- released a severe/tight breath
- exhale blew away strain/anger/the stress of the day
- air exploded/ruptured/blasted from his lungs

- relief whooshed from lungs
- ___ decompressed her lungs
- spewed breath from nose
- expelled a stormy bluster
- ___ left him in a windy bluster
- huffed out a peeved/humored breath
- thrust out a breath
- discharged/vented his lungs
- his exhale gusted/blew audibly
- surged/stormed a single exhale
- dumped a great breath
- ___ drove out a curt breath
- released breathy laugh/groan
- sharp/serrated/keen exhalation
- released an abrupt puff/whuff/swoosh of air
- air punched out of lungs
- breath exited in a rapid/brisk whoosh
- whizz/rush of air expelled from
- chest caved with an exhale
- breathed out relief/resignation
- a blow of air

- dispelled a lungful of grief/fury
- air burst from him
- wind knocked from lungs
- forced/pushed out an exhale
- ribs collapsed/fell in a turbulent exhale
- mighty/robust/hardy breath left him
- burst of air shot/spewed from his mouth

—ACTIVE BREATHING—

- recovered her breath
- breath resumed normal pattern
- tiny spurts of breath
- little panted breaths
- a murmur of breath
- breath high in the chest (shallow, panicked)
- breath lost depth
- labored breathing
- puffs of air fluttered her nostrils
- ribs rising in steady rhythm
- broad movement of her chest
- drew air in and out of his nose

- breathing deep/methodically/calmly through the nose
- moved air in and out of nose
- breathed slow with long/deliberate ins and outs
- heaved/billowed air
- air zipped over parted teeth
- breath grew/shrank
- open-mouthed breaths
- the balmy/hot gusts/waves of breath
- wheezed/whistled through the nose
- air left nostrils in rapid jets
- spewed in great surges
- lungs pumped hard
- a squall/storm of breaths
- shoulders heaved with
- angry/frightened/impassioned breaths
- lungs in high/rapid function
- breathed windstorms through nose
- surges of air worked his ribcage
- pulled draughts through her nostrils
- regulated/governed her erratic breath
- heaving chestfuls of air

- chased his breath
- ribs worked in great heaves
- heaves of wind dried his throat/nose/mouth
- breast rose and plummeted
- mass of his chest swelled/surged
- moved air through his lungs
- heightened/elevated/increased breath
- breath coming hard
- air left lungs in a surge of rage/shock
- exhaled fear/regret/anger
- rapid rise and fall of his shoulders
- breath stung/dried the walls of her throat

Breathing can be connected to internal (heart, pulse, thoughts) or external beats (clock, ocean waves, pounding tread).

Chapter Six: Internal Systems

—HEART, CHEST, and RIBS—

> Heartbeats and pulses can be felt in the chest, ears, head, hollow of the throat, ribs, or any pulse point.

Constricting or Freezing
- heart retracted/constricted
- heart lodged in her ribs
- chilled/wrung the heart
- heart locked/froze/stilled/stopped cold/cut out/drew up/quit
- heart dried up in his chest
- froze his heart midbeat/mid-thump
- heart vacated/abandoned its cavity/his chest
- ___ mined/dug the heart from his chest
- ___ hardened/pulsed in his chest
- ___ rusted/corroded her heart
- ___ squeezed tight/constricted about her heart

Rejoicing

- heart pranced/cartwheeled/summersaulted/made pirouettes
- heart trilled/sang with ___
- heart kicked up a happy/lively tango/salsa
- frolicking heart
- fuming tick/happy clicking of his heart
- joy/delight swelled/billowed her heart
- heart kicked up its heels

Skipping or Stuttering

- heart leapt/jerked against its tethers/reins
- heart turned or tipped over/flipped/pitched/listed/skipped/vaulted
- heart went arrhythmic/haywire
- heart stuttered/toppled/stammered
- a series of spluttering heartbeats/palpitations
- ___ sent a blip/glitch/hiccup to his heartbeat
- heart a pattery mess

- heart out of cadence/sync
- heart lost rhythm
- heart/cadence bordered on wild
- his rowdy/disorderly heart
- heart pattered an ailing/sickly rhythm
- heart snitched/stole/snagged/thieved an extra few beats
- heart tripped/stumbled out a frantic beat
- quiver/tremble of his heart

Speeding

- heart pitter-pattered against her ribcage
- rattled its cage/inside her
- ___ sprang heart into battle/fighting rhythm
- the drum of her heart
- a wild/dreadful timpani beat
- gunned into overdrive
- his heart sprang up to fight/battle/charge
- the rat-a-tat/jackhammering of her heart
- heart went on a spree/let loose
- rapid-fire heartbeats

- pulse/blood/heart pumping as if she had ___
- heart whirred on pace with
- a rampant/unbridled heart
- threw heart into high gear/speed
- heart pumped ragged breath
- uptick/upbeat of her heart
- heart picked up speed/quickened/fired up
- heart thrumming wildly/sluggishly
- heart in a spasm/in a throe of panic/in a frenzy
- heart doing crazy/wild/feral things in his chest/to his ribs
- beat like a rabbit's (or any other frightened animal)
- terror/delight licked at his heart
- heart punched/gave a kick
- crazed heart worked his lungs/drove his pulse
- ___ (emotion) rampaged/ran amok in his chest
- ribs laboring double-fast/-quick
- ribs working double-time/on the double
- chest throbbing violently/recklessly

- the gallop/canter/sprint of her heart
- heart burst into a jaunt/jog
- ___ spurred/startled her heart to a gallop
- the speedy clip/pace of his heartbeat
- listened to/felt the hammer/thundering of his heart
- ___ made her heart thrash
- his heart raged/threw a fit/worked itself up

Dropping or Vacating
- heart clunked/fell with a bang
- displaced/uprooted heart
- dropped to his stomach/down around his feet/half a foot
- caged heart thrashed/flailed to escape
- heart tried to get out of/beat its way through his ribcage/sternum
- heart clawed its way out
- ___ tore its way out of her chest
- heart in her throat
- heart clambered up her throat
- heart pounded in her throat
- sprinted up her throat

Hurting

- pinched ___ from her heart
- torqued the heart
- her writhing/squirming heart
- heart bruising/battering his ribs
- flame of ___ in his chest
- heart savaged/ravaged/pummeled his chest
- ___ strained sinews/chambers of her heart
- fear/anxiety burned a trail to her heart
- heart skinned/smarted
- ___ twisted in her breast
- made his heart a quivering burr/thorn in his chest
- the desolate/lonely cavity of his ribs
- fury glowed/burned red in his chest
- heart threw/dashed itself against her chest

Chest

- chest rose and fell
- chest bulged with purpose/affront
- chest tight with pain/panic
- bands tightened across his chest

- quaking deep beneath her ribs
- chest vibrated/rattled with her pounding heart
- ___ ached/tickled behind her sternum
- an ache lurked/prowled about her ribs
- his chest lost its puff/boast

_____

-Hearts can beam, cower, cry, dance, faint, frolic, roar, scowl, scream, smile, rear up, romp, wail, or any other personification.
-Hearts can (to show suppressed emotion) beam, frown, scowl, smile, etc.
-Hearts can feel like they'll break out/free, burst the chest, open, or rupture/splinter the ribs.
-Hearts can crack, shatter, splinter, or tear in two.

—PULSE, VEINS, BLOOD—

Slowing and Stopping
- ___ quieted/calmed her pulse
- beseeched/begged her pulse to calm/slow
- pulse dulled/mellowed/cooled/dimmed
- blood slowed its trek
- blood stopped pumping

- trickle of ___ moved through her veins
- blood stalled/suspended
- blood froze/went frosty/chilled/iced over
- blood turned sludgy/turned to mud in her veins
- made the blood curdle/congeal/spoil in his veins
- blood an icy sludge
- willed courage/strength into her blood

Faltering

- a thready pulse
- pulse skittered/staggered
- pulse tapped giddily/haphazardly/crazily
- ___ ruined the steady current/beat of her pulse
- ___ put a skitter in her pulse
- blood coursed chaotically through veins
- pulse went jagged

Surging

- pulse surged/quickened its throb
- felt a push of blood
- pulse skyrocketed/picked up

- ramped pulse into a thundering stampede/panic
- ___ ignited/sparked in/burned through his veins
- a rush of blood
- blood rushed in her ears
- sent her blood scrambling/into a tizzy
- ___ maddened/incensed her blood
- ___ tore through her veins
- furious/terrified blood jetted through
- his blood was up
- the heat of his blood
- blood violent in her body
- a blood-rioting ___
- blood a fiery liquid in his heart

Pounding

- thumping rhythm in her throat
- pulse struck his temple
- ___ powered the blood in his veins
- hammer blows of his pulse
- veins clogged/blazed with
- vein bulged over his temple and pulsed

- her blood a tattoo/rapping in her ears
- buffeted her eardrums
- pumped heat into muscles
- his pulse a whine/cry in his ear

-Blood itself can be angry, delirious, giddy, or any other emotion.
-Blood's flow can be compared to any water source (rivers, waterfalls, streams, arctic run-off, stagnant pond).
-Blood can bellow, scream, shriek, snarl, thunder, etc. (his blood snarled).
-For dramatic effect, the pulse can be felt in odd places (eyelids, spine, fingertips, etc.)

—STOMACH and CENTER—

→ Substitutes for *stomach*: belly, bowels, center, core, entrails, gut, innards, insides, interior, middle, midriff, soul, tummy

Burning or Freezing
- insides sparked with color/shades of
- fire in her belly/licking at her entrails

- something hot/frozen scurried through his belly
- ___ blistered/burned his stomach
- spread like ice through his innards
- ___ burned/scorched/braised the stomach

Coiling, Clenching, or Knotting
- stomach pitted into tight coils
- stomach clenched painfully
- ___ contracted his stomach
- a pang struck her middle
- innards clenched down
- entrails tied themselves in knots
- cords strung/pulled tight through her center
- ___ pinched his entrails
- stomach shrank in on itself
- gut contorted
- tummy knotted/fisted/kinked/tangled
- knots coiled in her belly
- ___ tied her tummy in knots
- bunched into a knot
- ___ tightened his gut
- rock formed in her stomach

Sinking

- innards sank to his knees
- a stone/brick dropped through his core
- a trap door in stomach gave way/fell open
- belly became a sinking stone
- stomach fell sharply/crashed/plummeted
- stomach sagged with understanding/dread
- stomach hollowed out

Rebelling

- stomach began a watery/slushy churn
- bile stirred/cycloned
- the acid of ___ regret/fear/etc.
- nausea frothed/foamed
- churned like spoiled/rancid meat in his gut
- sudden ailment/ache wrung his bowels
- ___ filled her stomach like the flu/a malady
- belly soured/gave a sick turn/fermented
- stomach churned a sour/an acidic brew

- bile threatened to vent/spew
- bile bubbled up/in her throat
- stomach rolled
- a malaise settled in
- ___ turned tummy upside down
- ___ inverted her stomach
- stomach heaved/churned/revolted
- stomach turned over/capsized/keeled over
- sudden malaise wrung/twisted his bowels
- insides tumbled into each other
- belly soured/fermented
- ___ pooled in stomach like acid

See also ACID IN THROAT (page 147).

Positive Emotion

- a ribbon of ___ twirled inside
- her insides performed a dance/jig/pirouette
- fillip of excitement in her middle
- ___ settled warm in his middle
- ___ warmed her insides
- rivulets of ___ in her belly

- ___ shot frissons through her center
- thrill of ___ zinged/tingled her tummy

Negative Emotion
- stomach a ruin of ___
- tornado/storm ripped through
- nerves danced in
- congealing/curdling stomach
- ___ was a lance/thrust to/pierce of his gut
- ___ socked/kicked her in the stomach
- ___ seized her gut
- innards heavy with ___
- ___ bled/tore through her middle
- lead/stone in the belly
- middle thickened/congealed uncomfortably
- ___ socked him in the stomach
- ___ battered her insides
- ___ slithered through his belly
- ___ billowed in his gut
- ___ cut him belly to sternum/ribs to spine
- ___ threatened his bowels
- bowels trembled violently

Flexible Emotion Beats

- belly felt a twinge of ___
- a kick/wallop of desire/fury in her middle
- stomach turned jittery
- ___ made his insides cheer/boo/rant/applause
- ___ squeezed his belly
- heartache/love expanded through her center
- insides wormed/fidgeted or wriggled/squirmed
- strange flopping in her belly

-Positive similes—birds, butterflies, feathers, fingerlings, tingles, minnows
-Negative similes—boulder, bricks, eels, maggots, spiders, stones, worms

Chapter Seven: Head

—MOTIONS—

Shaking
- sharp slice left and/then right
- shook her head in a swift arc
- wagged her head
- a quick no jerked his head
- swung his head in a no

Nodding
- gave a clipped nod
- nodded avidly/eagerly
- a single/sole/lone nod
- ducked her chin in agreement
- tight/curt/short/perfunctory nod
- bobbed her head
- nodded in long, contemplative lines
- tilted head in a yes
- dipped his chin in concession
- saluting/greeting tip of the head
- downward jut/jerk of the chin
- inclined his head in concession/recognition
- bowing head a touch
- agreeing plunge of the chin

- chin descended in a nod
- a vacant/unthinking nod
- nod of recognition/agreement/ farewell
- dipped/tipped/bowed his head once
- tipped his head forward
- jerked his chin in agreement

Rearing Back

- his head reared/jutted/went/ thrust/pitched back
- his chin jerked back/in
- ___ drove his head back

Turning Neck

- craned/cranked his neck about
- head swiveled on his shoulders
- swung to the side/whipped sideways
- turned with a snap of the neck
- looked over the shoulder
- glanced rearward/behind him
- cast a glower/smile back at

-See BODY MOVEMENT, TURNING (page 20) for more.

Tipping Sideways

→ Substitutes for *tipped*: angled, canted, cocked inclined, leaned, pitched, slanted, tilted, tipped

- put head to one side in a questioning/curious manner
- head inclined sideways
- head limped/hung/fell/dropped to one side
- a tilt-headed look at
- head at an oblique angle
- sloped his head to the left
- head bobbed to the side

-See BODY MOVEMENT, LEANING (page 23) for more.

—FACIAL EXPRESSIONS—

→ Substitutes for *face*: aspect, comportment, countenance, demeanor, expression, features, mien, visage

Flexible Emotion Beats
- his thinking/amused/ angry face
- the landscape of his face said/looked
- face rumpled with ___
- skin tightened over his face

- face closed down
- face opened wide with ___
- face screwed into a grimace/scowl
- scrunched up her features
- made/pulled a face that said
- the play of his countenance said ___
- host of emotions crisscrossing his face
- ___ smacked her face
- ___ sat lightly on her face
- he had ___ in his aspect (vengeance, love, etc.)
- her visage spelled ___
- ___ pinwheeled across her face
- face an impermeable/unreadable mask
- look of ___ passed over her features
- ___ play/range of emotions in her demeanor
- ___ clouded his expression
- flash of ___ on her face
- face glowed/gleamed/blazed with ___
- face carved into unforgiving/tormented lines

- shadow of ___ darkened her visage
- expression bordered on/resembled ___
- face hardened/wiped clear with a veil of ___
- ___ tangled her brow/the muscles of her face
- ___ passed/glided/floated over his face
- her countenance one of ___
- his expression folded/narrowed/closed with ___
- ___ shaped/molded/rewrote his features
- she shaped her face with ___
- her expression a question/exclamation mark
- ___ owned/overtook her features
- ___ circled/encompassed/orbited her face
- a ___ look outfitted him/dressed his face
- ___ misshaping/contorting his features
- features drew tight/went lax with ___
- countenance lively/alive/dead with ___

- ___ disoriented/confused his expression
- face crimping to contain ___
- ___ carved ruts into his face
- ___ recast her features
- ___ flitted/flashed/flickered across her face
- face fell/went slack
- expression dulled/crashed
- face contracted into tight lines
- ___ softened the harshness of his face

Eyebrows and Forehead

Brows Up

- eyebrows jogged up his forehead
- flicked both brows up
- eyebrows jumped/leapt up
- one ___ brow lifted
- raised a challenging/snarky eyebrow
- popped in eyebrow
- eyebrows went skyward
- eyebrows sat near/strained for her hairline
- one eyebrow edged/crept toward her hairline

- reached/stretched for his hairline
- brows stabbed/sloped high
- rose in a slow arch
- upward launch of eyebrows
- brows curved in surprise/with a dare
- one brow winged up
- twitch of the eyebrow

Brows Down

- brows perched low
- eyebrows folded down
- screwed brows lower
- brows cut/positioned low
- brow muscles bunched low
- downward V of his brow
- brows slung low
- brows curled down

Brows Together

- brows compressed/met over his eyes
- brows twitched/reached toward each other
- eyebrows collided in the center/above his nose
- eyebrows melted together
- eyebrows crashed in the middle

- narrowed her brows
- lines inscribed into/appeared on the space above nose
- parallel lines formed over bridge of nose
- valley carved/chiseled into the flesh between his eyes
- eyebrows moved into/stayed in a ___ position
- brows a ___ slash above eyes
- eyebrows fitted in a stern/strict line

Forehead

- wrinkle cut across/bridged the expanse of her forehead
- brow constricted
- wrinkle lines assembled on/crowded her forehead
- concern/doubt pinched her forehead in the middle
- forehead pressed down
- creases amassed on/flocked together on her forehead
- ridges scored/etched into the flesh above his eyes
- a troubled/concerned/ questioning brow
- his brow a thundercloud

- forehead a map/maze of wrinkles
- ___ hardened his brow
- line/groove slashed across his forehead
- brow darkened/clouded with
- worry knot/s on the brow

_____
_____
_____
_____
_____
_____
_____
_____
_____
_____
_____
_____
_____
_____
_____
_____
_____

-A brow can arch, carve ruts, crease, crinkle, crouch, crumple, dome, etch, furrow, gather, groove, inscribe, pucker, purse, ruck, rumple, rut, score.
-Eyebrows can arch, bury together, cinch, curve, ease apart, flicker, hunch, invert, knit, perk up, plunge earthward, pull in, pump suggestively, settle over eyes, slam/tug together, slice/pluck downward, take the shape of ___ [emotion], twitch up/down, waggle, weave.

Chapter Eight: Eyes

→ Substitutes for *eyes*: depths, globes, orbs, peepers, seas/pools, wells

→ Substitutes for *looked*: be aware of, beheld, checked out, detected, discovered, examined, eyed, found, gaped, gawked, gazed, glanced, glared, glimpsed, inspected, kept an eye on, monitored, noticed, observed, peeked, peeped, peered, scrutinized, searched, sighted, spotted, spied, stared, studied, surveyed, took note of, viewed, watched, witnessed

—BASIC ACTIONS—

Unfocused

→ Substitutes for *unfocused*: bland, blank, dead-eyed, deadpan, detached, dim, dull, emotionless, empty, expressionless, flat, flat-eyed, glassy, glazed/glazing, guarded, hollow, inane, lax, level, over, remote, sightless, slack, unfixed, unfocused, unspeaking, untethered, vacant, vacuous

- stared into the middle-distance _____
- gaze going remote _____
- expression went vacuous _____
- ___ made his eyes wide and blank _____
- eyes hollowed out _____

Narrowing

→ Substitutes for *narrowed*: aslant, constricted, contracted, cramped, hooded, slanted, slatted, slit-eyed, slitted, sloped, squinched, squint-eye, squinted, tapered

- eyes tightened at the corners
- eyed him narrowly
- shot him a narrow look
- made slits of her eyes
- gave a narrow-eyed look
- hardened her lids
- eyelids at half-mast
- eyes closed midway
- squinty-eyed
- eyes crinkled to slits
- half-closed eyes
- hooded eyes
- lids crescent in a squint
- narrowed her lashes
- ___ thinned her eyes
- heavy-lidded gaze
- low-lashed gaze
- slanted him a ___ look
- cocked an eye half open

Widening

→ Substitutes for *wide/widened* or *deep* as relates to eyes or gazes: big, boundless, cavernous, enormous, flared, immense, oversized, prodigious, vast, voluminous

- wide-eyed countenance
- lashes flipped full-open
- round-eyed expression
- blue/brown eyes framed in white
- eyes flashed open wide
- eyes splayed/torn wide
- shot open
- doubled in size
- her big eyes
- lashes flew high
- eyelids stretched wide
- eyes telegraphed/broadcast surprise
- the whites of his eyes visible
- eyes gaped
- ___ brightened the whites of her eyes
- blinked excessively/slowly (speed of blinks conveys emotion)
- eyes took up his whole face

Closing and Opening

→ Substitutes for *close*: clench, draw down, fasten, shut, shutter

→ Substitutes for *open*: crack, fissure, hoist, lift, raise, throw wide, uncover, unshut

- lids trembled/floated downward
- lids slammed shut
- eyelids tipped closed
- lids pinched tight
- veiled eyes behind lashes
- let eyelids slide down/slip shut
- scrunched eyes shut
- lids came down
- flipped her lashes down
- resealed her lids
- lashes swept shut/up
- eyes crammed tight
- eyes winched shut
- lashes shadowed cheekbones
- eyelids drooped
- drifted closed
- eyelids hovered low
- lashes lowered/shaded her cheeks/shielded his eyes
- quinched/crammed her eyes shut

- lifted her lashes
- lashes shot upward
- his lids lifted to
- lashes flicked up
- lids blinked open
- eyes flung open

Side Eye

→ Substitutes *sideways* (glance): askance, oblique, side-on, sidelong, sideward, sideways, sidelong shift

- tossed her the side-eye
- she side-eyed him
- eyed him side-on/cornerwise
- looked at him through side-eyes
- shot a glance from the corner of his eye
- her side vision took in
- glanced at him sidelong

—EMOTION in the EYES—

Positive Emotion
- a glint/light touched his eyes
- sparkled with laughter/challenge

- eyes soft as a whisper/breeze/ the scent of rain
- soft-as-silk gaze
- eyes crinkled with a smile
- laugh creases/lines around his eyes
- depth of her gaze (bottomless, fathomless)

Negative Emotion
- ___ clouded/hooded/fogged his eyes
- eyes like balls of fire
- spark of ___ ignited in his eyes
- poison-tipped gaze
- snapped him a look
- cut her a glare
- her eyes slammed into
- shot him a dirty/nasty look/glare
- hit him with a fierce/fiery look
- stiffened her gaze
- burning eyes directed at
- levied a glare
- eyes like hot coals/embers
- eyes bulging with ___
- a daggered/bladed/knifing look/glare
- eyes spewed/gushed/hurled ___

- light went out of his eyes
- glimmer in her eyes extinguished
- ___ snuffed/extinguished/cut/severed from his eyes
- wielded her most haughty/cutting glare
- her gaze gutted/emptied him
- eyes flattened/shut him out
- muscle twitched/ticked under/beside his eye
- his eyes snapped at her
- eyes burned fury-hot
- sent a stink-eye
- fire glittered in her eyes/expression
- eyes had a dark/sinister light
- ___-dimmed/___-brightened eyes
- a fire started/fizzled in his eyes
- pupils dilated/flared with rage
- his sight was peppery/fiery on her
- hard-as-hate eyes
- the stab/prick/thrust of his gaze
- the stone/iron/ice/in his gaze
- eyes sharp as glass/thorns/nails/fractured stone

- penetrated/pervaded her with a look of ___
- stabbed/pinned/pegged him with a ___ look
- skewered him with a hot gaze
- his thorny/barbed/bristly/briery look
- eyes guttered with pain
- eyes like two chips of flint/steel

Flexible Emotion Beats
- ___ rose/flickered in her eyes
- ___ vivified/enlivened/revived his eyes
- ___ written in his eyes
- ___ stirred behind his eyes
- ___ ruled/dominated the glance she sent
- ___ look coasted over her eyes
- ___ played/waged in the backs of his eyes
- ___ lustered/burnished his eyes
- ___ bled/dripped/seeped from his eyes
- ___ look came into/left his eyes
- ___ hovered in/hung about his gaze

- ___ retreated from her eyes
- put ___ into his eyes
- her eyes registered ___
- eyes donned a supernatural/otherworld luster
- a haze/fog of ___ swimming in her eyes
- her look heavy with ___
- a burst of ___ lit his eyes
- her look turned ___ (deadpan, snappish, comical)
- inflexible/pliant eyes
- solidified her gaze with ___
- something ___ in his look/eyes
- his eyes bathed her in ___
- gaze clawed into her/scratched through his resolve
- hard/wide/admiring eyes adorned his face
- a tease/threat squinted his eyes
- a welcoming/rejecting gaze
- communicated a look of ___

-Eyes/gazes can perform actions such as blister, build (a bridge, a wall), enslave, excavate, peel, run from/to, strut like a cock, suck the life from, suffocate, soothe, etc.
-A stare or look can be as simple as "strong" or "weak," "mild" or "angry."
-Merge the senses: gazes can smell foul or sweet; they can be tactile (slippery, sticky, rough); eyes can leer or smirk.
-Eyes can ask, beg, say, etc. (His eyes begged understanding.)

—LOOKING TO or AWAY—

Looking To
- traded a glance with
- their eyes linked
- he rested his eyes on her
- favored him with a ___ look/stare
- her eyes darted between his
- a ___ look crawled/danced between them
- his raking/roving gaze
- she tapped/nudged him with her gaze
- his gaze aligned with/attached to hers
- his ___ gaze awaited hers

- braved his gaze
- ___ flung his gaze around
- she met him in the eye/she met his ___ gaze
- she blinked over to him
- her gaze fell on/slipped to his
- his startled/amused eyes swung her way
- their eyes came back to him
- she showed/flashed him her ___ eyes
- met each other's questioning look
- she put him in her eyeline
- gave him a look layered with
- eyes pinging to
- cut his eyes to
- swiveled ___ eyes to
- of their own accord, his eyes went to
- turned his ___ eyes toward
- trained her gaze on
- skidded/skipped a glance her way
- shifted her eyes around the room
- the flit/skip of his eyes brought them to
- rapt attention hopping between

- gaze bounced from ___ to ___
- eyes came at him with
- eyes changed focus to
- a double take rotated his head
- gaze homed in on
- eyes honed to
- his ___ eyes belonged to
- stole a glance at
- a skim of the eye
- darted a glance
- her vision planted on
- watched from under his brow
- thrust gaze up at
- capped eyes on
- punctured him with a glare
- inched his eyes toward
- eyes pitching toward
- pitched ___ eyes to/at
- lobbing him a look of
- turned a ___ eye at/on him
- gave her cynical/trusting/sleepy gaze to him
- snapped eyes up from
- ___ drew her regard
- threw a look her way
- the black/blue/green of her eyes flashed to

- aimed her eyes at
- took a gander of
- yanked/jerked his eyes back to
- gaze moved to
- gave it a once-over
- sight traveled over
- his roving/wandering eyes caught up to
- looked through her lashes
- looked through the bottoms/tops of her eyes

Looking Away
- shriveled/shrank back from his gaze
- turned the back of her head to him
- the line of his sight fell/drifted
- he felled/dropped/sank his gaze
- eyes downcast
- he tore/ripped from her pleading/teary eyes
- eyes fidgeted/squirmed
- adjusted her view downward/away

Locking On
- eyes tangled/twined with/ untangled from hers

- pinned her with a ___ lens
- sight/attention riveted on
- stared at him with her ___ eyes
- anchored/bound her gaze to his
- couldn't sever the line/tether of her gaze
- his gaze gripped/clamped onto hers
- his gaze caught/ensnared her
- his eyes stationed on her
- ___ latched/affixed their gazes
- his eyes locked her down/in place
- drilled his gaze into hers
- he connected/coupled their eyes
- felt skewered by/impaled with his gaze
- fixed him with a ___ look
- their eyes engaged/battled
- the burning tether/shackle of his gaze
- in the orbit/domain of his gaze
- gazes met/joined in an implacable lock

- maintained flawless/shaky connection
- bound her with an immutable/deadly stare

> A gaze can court, flirt, or marry another's.

—SEEKING—

→ Substitutes for *search*: canvassed, foraged, hunted for, pursued, ransacked, rummaged, scavenged, scoured, scouted, scrounged, sought, swept, tracked down, trailed after

- gaze flitting about her environs
- eyes panned the landscape
- a visual sweep of
- a sweeping glance
- cast her eyes around
- moved his eyes in a slow arc
- his gaze hunted ___
- her sight went far
- her roving/questing eyes
- copped a look

—EXAMINING—

- he took her measure
- sized her up

- scoped her out
- eyes gobbled her/it up
- took stock of her
- burrowing gaze
- he catalogued/canvassed/ appraised/regarded her
- her gaze tight on
- eyes snaked along
- considered her long and hard
- gripped it with his eyes
- took inventory of
- passed/gave her a searching/ exploratory look
- trawled his gaze down her
- eyes bored through her
- critically scanned
- narrow-eyed scrutiny
- his gaze delved deep
- her sight meandered his features
- assayed her from the bottoms/sides of his eyes

—LASHES and BLINKING—

- lashes beat softly
- stunned flitter of her lashes

- palpebral twitches
- fanned/fluttered her lashes
- blinked ___ from her eyes
- a beat of the eyelids
- blinked owlishly/an owl's blink
- eyes closed for a lengthy blink
- a surrendering blink
- vested her with a wink
- looked through the fringe of her lashes

—TEARS—

- contained the cry within her mouth/behind her teeth
- bit lip to contain
- killed the wail
- held tears at bay
- tears leaked
- wet skipped down her cheeks
- she welled up
- eyes brimmed
- swimming eyes
- moisture threatened
- eyes misted over
- went misty-eyed
- glimmer of unshed tears
- fogged his vision

- stinging filled her eyes
- eyes glossed over
- silent tears rolled
- glassy eyes
- an errant/rogue tear
- a squelched sob
- her eyes filmed
- watery vision
- squeezed from the corner of her eyes
- tears strained at her eyes
- tears pooled/puddled up
- tears pushed against eyes/lids
- blinked eyes to keep tears in place/to sidetrack tears
- cry rose within
- got choked up/choked back sob
- dismembered/dismantled a building cry
- huge/luminescent with unshed tears
- her flooded/brimming eyes
- tears blinded/impaired her eyes
- precarious hold on a deluge of tears
- her fuzzing/fogging/swimming gaze
- eyes awash/liquifying

- moisture spilled over the rim/through lashes
- a mournful glistening in the eyes
- a burn flared behind his eyelids
- eyes pinched with tears
- tear-brightened/darkened lashes
- watered and overflowed
- despair eked from her eyes
- drip/tear surmounted the bridge of her nose
- tears snagged/garbled her words
- tear-burned eyes
- spine-shuddering sob built
- ___ germinated a sob
- tears breached her lids
- moisture flooded
- tears distorted her world
- sob lashed her chest
- tears pumped out
- water rimmed/bordered/lined his eyelids
- sobs wrenched/racked her innards
- a burn at the borders of her eyes

- burned the back of the throat
- glint of tears
- tears gummed up her throat
- screamed/shrieked a cry
- humiliating/snot-filled honk
- moisture accumulated/collected in his eyes
- lids beat tears into retreat
- pricking/pressure built behind her lids
- tears pressed behind his eyelids
- wetness gathered in eyes/on lashes
- swallowed tears
- ran down the back of her nose/throat
- blinked a tear free
- tear-stained sight
- salt on the lips
- tears tracked/chased one another down her cheeks
- blinding tears

-Chin and lips can tremble with tears.
-See SADNESS/CRYING in TAGS (page 176) for substitutes for *tears*.

Chapter Nine: Nose and Ears

—NOSE—

→ Substitutes for *flared*: blowing wide, broadened, bulged, distended, enlarged, expanded, sprawled, splayed, swelled, went wide, widened, yawned

Nostrils Widening
- wind-gusting nostrils
- nostril-flaring distemper/desire
- blew through her nostrils
- nostrils blowing wide
- nostrils enlarged/spread wide/broadened
- nostrils fat with anger

Miscellaneous Beats
- screwed up her nose/face
- sniffed dismissively/ reproachfully at
- sniffed and made a face
- tic plucked at his nostrils
- turned her nose in the air
- twitched her nose (disdain)
- wrinkled/crinkled her nose at him

- pinched the bridge of his nose
- quivering/fluttering nostrils
- grunted through nostrils

Smell

→ Substitutes for *scent*: aroma, bouquet, essence, fragrance, odor, perfume, redolence, smell, stench, stink, tang

- odor hit high in the nose
- nostrils twitched, scenting
- stench forced itself to the back of his tongue/down his throat
- drowned her lungs in scent
- odor stuffed/rammed itself up her nose
- aroma coated/sweetened/burned the tongue
- odor stung his nostrils
- scent registered
- encompassed him with the scent of
- odor snagged her senses
- scent rode the wind/infiltrated the breeze
- the perfume of ___ accompanied
- breathed in the aroma
- caught a whiff of

- a draught of ___ scent
- air thick with the tang of
- scent commanded/hijacked the room
- odor engorged/engulfed the air
- the scent entered/invaded him
- fragrance washed over her
- stink wafted off him
- nostrils picked up/sensed
- took in the scent of
- ___ reached his nose
- nose led him to
- drank in the aroma of
- drew in the essence
- ___ carried the bouquet of
- lifted her nose to the fragrance
- ___ raised the scent of
- stench hit her
- nose to the wind
- air perfumed by
- odor stuffed into her nostrils

Scents can do the following to the nostrils: assail, assault, bite, burn, coat, fill, flood, meet, rouse (hunger/memories), smart in, sting, tease, tickle, violate.

—EARS and HEARING—

- tuned/primed/honed her ears
- within earshot
- hearing homed in on
- pricked his ears for the sound
- cocked an ear
- strained to listen
- leaned forward at her words
- sound met/rose to her ears
- noise seeped into her hearing
- listened with half an ear
- half listened
- sound can

Sounds can do the following to the ears, eardrums, or hearing: abrade, assault, brush, buffet, caress, chafe, dawn on, elude, escape, flood, grate, kiss, pierce, punch, pummel, register, rub wrong, scrape/rake against, sink in, slam into, strike, stroke, tap, tease, tickle, touch, toy with, trickle in

Chapter Ten: Mouth, Teeth, and Tongue

—MOUTH—

Bunched Mouth
- mouth in a judging/teasing wad
- mouth pinched
- cockled/pursed his lips
- bunched his mouth into a pucker
- ___ wadded her mouth
- mouth screwing hard/tight
- mouth tightened
- clenched mouth
- jutted/poked out his lips
- mouth worked into a bitter/dubious pucker

Flat Mouth
- mouth a straight/crinkled line
- flat-lipped silence
- blanched/bloodless/pale/pallid lips
- mouth pressed into a bloodless/white line
- the ___ set of her mouth/mouth set with
- mouth compressed
- ___ thinned/flattened her mouth

Miscellaneous Beats
- folded her lips shut
- ___ ruffled her lips
- folds bracketed his mouth
- lips flopped apart (see JAW, SAGGING [pg. 142] for more gaping)
- chewed her lip/the corner of her mouth
- sucked her lower lip between her teeth
- mouth tucked (uncertain)
- mouth wobbled/lips trembled
- ___ made a dry pit/desert in his mouth

—TEETH—

→ Substitutes for *grinding*: grating, scraping, gnashing, gritting

- teeth bore down on the inside of his cheek
- teeth worried/pinched/trapped her lower lip
- bore his teeth into his lip
- lip white beneath the pressure of teeth
- ___ drove her lip between

- her teeth
- glided her teeth over her bottom lip
- lips drawn/mashed between his clamped teeth
- lip snatched/slipped between her teeth
- clamped his tongue between his teeth
- sucked his teeth/canine
- ran a tongue over the edges of his teeth
- buffed/polished teeth with the tongue
- tongue swept the fronts of her teeth
- bared his teeth
- ___ rattled/clattered her teeth
- teeth all a-rattle
- fastened her clacking teeth
- teeth banged together
- ___ made her teeth ache/molars scrape
- set his teeth on edge
- molars squeaking together
- teeth welded together
- teeth rasped against each other
- ___ set her teeth to grinding
- set her teeth against

- locked his molars
- ground his back teeth together
- clenched teeth
- clamped her teeth tight
- teeth cracked together
- ___ made the roots of her teeth twinge
- hurt/cold to the roots of her teeth
- report of teeth snapping shut (see JAW [pg. 141] for more closing teeth)
- click of her teeth
- teeth shut tight against

—TONGUE—

Wet/Dry
- flashed tongue over upper lip
- dampened lips
- moistened dry teeth with a swipe of the tongue
- tongue swabbed nervously
- tip of his tongue ran between lips
- darting tongue laid moisture along the lips
- slid his tongue/ran a slow trail between his lips

- parched tongue cleaved to the roof of her mouth
- her tongue a desert/wasteland/an arid plain
- tongue pasted/stuck/cemented to teeth
- scraped dry tongue over lips
- tongue sticky in her mouth
- tongue felt like sandpaper/concrete/dry bread
- worked tongue over thirsty lips
- swollen/bloated/puffy tongue

See also DRYNESS IN THROAT (page 146).

Speaking Tongue
- question popped from his tongue
- the word a jagged whisper on his tongue
- moved his tongue in a hush
- words drained/dripped off her tongue
- tongue had a mind of its own
- her barbed-wire/double-edged tongue
- the sharp/razored/serrated side of the tongue

- said with a tongue that could cut glass/clip a hedge/shear a sheep
- a vicious wield of the tongue
- a curse hot on his tongue
- words heated/developed on her tongue
- a sputter on his tongue
- the word meandered/wandered off her tongue
- words bulky/awkward on his tongue
- wrapped his tongue around the truth/word
- tongue tiptoed/tangled around the words
- words fit nicely around her tongue/in her mouth
- words on the tip of his tongue
- tongue set off/took off in babbling speech
- retort came/leapt to his tongue
- he found his tongue
- tripped on her tongue

Unspeaking Tongue

- swallowed words sprouting on the tongue
- tongue burned with the urge to speak

- words queued up in the throat
- words eager to fly from the tongue
- sliced/cut the words from/off her tongue
- kept his tongue in check
- bridled/curbed/bit/minded his tongue
- pinched his rogue/errant tongue between teeth
- teeth caught his tongue
- lame tongue couldn't produce words
- tongue a useless accessory
- tongue on strike/went limp
- tongue-tied
- swallowed her tongue
- frozen/paralyzed tongue
- words languished/died on her tongue
- ___ drove the words from his tongue
- words trembled on her tongue
- tongue refused the words
- stunted tongue
- tongue staggered/faltered/dithered
- ___ bound/locked his tongue

- an enslaved/captive tongue
- tongue frozen to the floor/roof of her mouth
- tongue stuck at the corner of her mouth

Miscellaneous Beats

- ___ (emotion) flooded her mouth/ washed her tongue
- clicked/clucked his tongue
- emotion swelled at the back of her tongue
- ___ coated his tongue in bitterness
- regret/anticipation touched the tongue with a sour/sweet flavor
- tongue poked the inside of her cheek
- jutted his tongue into his cheek/from his mouth
- tongue peeked between her lips/at the corner
- ___ pooled on his tongue (an emotion or saliva)

-Tongues can be barbed, befuddled, callous, cruel, curt, dead, deceptive, lashing, loosened, mute, naughty, nimble, sharp, silent, slick, sluggish, smooth, sneaky, snippy, stupid, unhinged, unruly, unspeaking, wagging, warped, and endless more.

-The tongue can dart, flash, flick, glance, pass, roll, slick, sweep, swipe, or trace over lips.

Chapter Eleven: Smiles

—SMILING VERBS—

→ Substitutes for *mouth*: face, features, expression, lips

→ Substitutes for *smile* and *grin*: amusement, banter, charm, cheer, contentment, delight, drollery, elation, enjoyment, excitement, gaiety giddiness gladness glee, happiness, high spirits, humor, joy, play, playfulness, merriment, mirth, pleasure, rapture, satisfaction, serenity, simper, thrill, wonder

→ Substitutes for *corners of the mouth*: edges, ends, folds, seams, sides

→ These lists are also useful for frowns.

Verbs for Character or Emotion Controlling the Smile

- allowed
- ambushed
- arranged
- bared teeth
- beamed
- broke into
- contemplated
- cracked
- crooked
- doubled
- earned
- eased into
- fashioned
- fastened on
- formed
- gave
- gleamed
- hoisted
- imparted
- let go
- molded
- mustered
- offered
- presented

- produced
- ramped
- relaxed
- repaid
- sent
- sent back
- shot
- shone
- showered
- sketched on
- spawned
- spread
- sprung
- tacked on
- threw on
- twinned
- worked/worked up
- yielded

Example beats:
- relaxed into a smile
- locked a grin on
- repaid the grin with one of his own
- pulled a slow smile
- beamed her gratitude
- twinned his broad smile
- allowed a crinkle of a smile
- worked up a cocky grin
- spawned a smile of
- formed a cheeky smile
- developed her smile into one of
- offered up a grin
- let go of a smirk
- brought a smile to bear
- wielded a battering ram/sledgehammer of a smile
- contemplated an upward slant of the lips
- doubled his smile
- sprung a grin
- ambushed him with a ___ smile
- smile had a ___ aspect to it

Verbs for Smile Controlling the Character

- appeared on
- alighted on
- appropriated
- begged for release
- bent
- birthed on
- bled over lips
- bowed
- budded
- burned bright
- carried
- chiseled onto
- cinched
- climbed up
- came over
- contained
- covered
- crept
- crossed
- curved
- curled
- danced
- drew up
- dominated
- dusted
- ferried lips into
- erupted
- flickered
- flirted with
- folded
- formed on
- graced
- inched
- jotted across
- kicked up
- lifted
- made a line across
- matured on
- moved on/into over/across
- overtook
- pinched
- poked
- pulled
- pushed cheeks skyward/upward
- plucked
- quivered across
- quirked
- rippled
- rounded
- ruffled

- sat on
- scratched at
- seized
- shifted
- shimmied up
- slid
- slashed
- slouched
- soaked up
- splayed across
- split lips
- sprung
- stalked
- swathed
- swung free
- took residence/ possession/custody
- tweaked
- teased
- threatened
- ticked
- tickled
- tipped
- touched
- toyed with
- turned
- turned up/down
- twisted
- twitched
- upturned
- warbled
- writhed

_____
_____
_____
_____
_____
_____
_____
_____
_____
_____
_____
_____
_____
_____
_____
_____
_____
_____
_____
_____
_____
_____

Example Beats:

- grin sprang across her face
- smile jotted across her lips
- smile alive/bubbling with
- smile was a ___ thing/creature
- folded the skin around the mouth
- contentment hooked his mouth
- mirth soaked up his expression
- face/expression lifted
- mouth carried a ___ smile
- smile crawled up her face
- a shark's/wolf's smile
- smile full of/teemed with falsehood/mischief
- smile crossed/traversed/covered her lips
- smile stalked/hunted her
- smile ambushed/assailed her
- smile breezed over her
- gentleness/humor touched her lips
- smile ruffled his lips
- sat loose on his mouth
- lips held a smile loosely/tightly
- lips kicked up
- lips danced around a smile

—SMIRKS—

→ Substitutes for *smirk*: leer, simper, sneer
→ Useful smirking verbs: slanted, sloped, tilted, tipped

- one-sided smile/pluck of the lips
- wry smile
- sly grin
- half-smile
- half-cocked smile
- sideways smile
- wonky smile
- lifted on one side
- angled mouth/grin
- shrugged one corner
- cockeyed/uneven smile
- quirked his lips
- slid/pushed a smirk up one half of his face
- crooked smile/smug look
- hooked up on one side
- warp of his lips
- sloped mouth/grin
- uptick of one corner
- swoop to one side
- the slide of her mouth
- torqued her lips at him

- one corner inched up/dragged upward
- smile leaned on half of her mouth
- grinned from one corner of his mouth
- bother/mirth tipped one side of his mouth
- spread a sneer across his lips
- smug slide of her mouth
- lips twisted to the side
- tilt to his mouth when he spoke
- his grin skewed
- lips squirmed to the side
- smile walked up one side of his face
- smug purse of the lips
- tweaked her lips to the side
- bunched one cheek
- smile turned crooked
- one side of his lips pulled/curved into a grin
- pursed/pulled her lips to the side
- sneer pulled at his cheek
- let one side curl up
- ___ brought a twist/leer/grin to his lips

—HALF SMILES—

- gave a partial/quasi-smile
- half-done/baked/made smile
- the shaving/slice/sliver of a smile
- a thin smile
- smile with no teeth
- smiled thinly
- cracked a smile
- start/bud of a smile
- smile nascent on her
- hint/trace of a smile touched/brushed his lips
- a little/trifle smile came to her
- a ghost of a smile
- smile warbled her mouth
- dawning of a smile
- lines pulled at the corners of his mouth
- lips tweaked/twitched/tugged
- mouth played at smiling
- smile shadowed her mouth
- teeth peeked through lips

—FAKE and CONTAINED SMILES—

- facsimile of a smile
- trawled up a smile
- pasted on a smile
- stuck a ___ smile on her face
- pulled lips back from his teeth
- showed her teeth
- forced a ___ smile
- his not/non-smile
- chiseled a smile into features
- allowed a smile to peek from behind
- conceded a smile
- grid her teeth into a smile
- a set smile
- the effigy/semblance of a smile
- lips pinched upward (tension)
- smile felt strained
- mouth-only smile
- found a ___ smile for him
- dragged a smile up from
- ___ won her a smile
- a complimentary grin
- snarled a smile
- rolled lips to contain a smile

- prevented a grin from curving
- pressed lips inward
- bit back a grin
- swallowed a smile
- wrestled/subdued a smile
- reapplied his smile

> See FAKE in THESAURUS (page 164) for helpful adjectives.

—FULL SMILES—

- a perfect/crooked rank of teeth
- grinned with all his teeth
- showed rows of teeth
- smile showed a full grid of teeth
- displayed teeth in a ___ grin
- teeth shone pearly through his grin
- smile to suit an alligator/viper/cat
- ___ grin exposed his teeth
- showed him a full rack of teeth
- sun/joy shone in her smile
- smile swung free
- smiled so big it broke/split her face
- undiluted/full-strength smile

- teeth flashed, white and broad
- smile expanded to reveal canines
- smiled a cramp into cheek
- white crescent/half-moon of a smile
- smile eased wide
- face-splitting grin

Chapter Twelve: Laughter and Frowns

—LAUGHTER—

→ Substitutes for *laugh/laughter*: amusement, cackled, chortled, chuckled, giggled, glee, guffawed, hilarity, hooted, hysteria, snickered, sniggered, tittered, mirth, scoffed

Sound Qualities
- snorted/barked a laugh
- bark/snort of a laugh
- snorted through her laughter
- hooted a laugh
- chirped/cheeped a laugh
- gurgled/bubbled with laughter
- grunted a laugh
- rumbled from the base/depths of his chest
- huffed/scoffed/coughed out a laugh
- two-note/single-note laugh
- chuckle quaked/shivered/stuttered its way out
- her laughter was a ___ (bell, honk, rippling stream, etc.)
- deep, gurgling laughter

-Textures of laughter: airy, breathy, blustery, boyish, chesty, croaky, deep-barreled, deep-chested, deep/low-throated, feminine, graveled, girlish, hoarse, husky, masculine, nosy, raspy, scratchy, smoky, throaty, windy.
-Combo laughs: cringe-laugh, grunt-laugh, huff-laugh, laugh-choke, snort-laugh

Quiet

- a laughing huff of air
- gentle puff of a laugh
- light strains of laughter
- her breath the outline/semblance of a laugh
- chuffed with laughter
- laughter sprinkled the air
- laughed lightly/gently/mildly/daintily/delicately/neatly
- abdomen pulsed with a hint of laughter
- sparse laughter
- blew a laugh from his nose
- uttered a small/little/soft/hushed laugh
- rendered a light laugh
- sweet laugh on her lips
- muted/dampened laugh

- throat resonated with low laughter
- laughter drifted/floated from her throat
- breathed a laugh through his nose
- snickered under her breath
- gentle laugh tickled her throat
- chuckle breathed from her
- took up giggling
- tittered a laugh
- ___ reared/birthed a chortle
- laughter burbled/bubbled in her throat
- two notes of a chuckle
- slow, deep laugh
- quiet laugh shivered out of her
- laughter was low and ___ (caustic/sultry)
- whispered laughter

Loud

- amusement rippled/undulated his abdomen
- string/chain/thread of laughter
- rising/escalating mirth
- riotous with laughter
- belted/trilled a laugh
- liberal/hacking laughter

- mouthful of laughter
- mouth was full of laughter
- mouth-splitting/open-mouthed laughter
- he cracked up
- big, obnoxious guffaw
- ripped out a laugh
- laughed full and long
- all-right/outright laughter
- hysteria rolled through her
- laughed aloud/out loud
- let laughter billow/surge/balloon
- resounded a ___ laugh
- trumpeted a laugh
- a fit of laughter
- rang out clear across
- peal of laughter
- bellowed/brayed a laugh
- blared/boomed with hilarity
- squealed with laughter
- a shriek of laughter
- doubled/amplified her laughter
- sent him into stitches
- shoulders/chest shook with laughter
- stomach bounced with laughter

- shuddered her ribcage/rattled her chest
- guffaws rocked him
- shuddered with laughter
- shook/trembled/roiled with laughter
- threw/tipped head back and hooted
- rippled from her throat
- laughter came in waves
- let it stem into a full-blown laugh
- doubled over with hilarity
- laughed with big body/belly chuckles
- full-belly laughter

Unexpected

(laughter taking control)
- laughter sprayed/showered spit
- a crack/shot/shout of laughter
- nosey chuckle escaped
- laughter charged out of him
- laughter stormed/left her throat
- erupted/exploded in laughter
- a laugh sprang from her
- a laugh found its way out
- surprised himself by laughing

- chest filled with laughter
- a curt/unexpected laugh left him
- vagrant laugh cut/tore from him
- laugh broke free of her throat
- careened up her throat
- burst into a laugh
- abrupt laugh wrenched from him
- explosion of inappropriate laughter
- a ___ laugh parted his lips/split his mouth wide
- a laugh burst open her mouth
- laughter demanded/pushed to escape her chest
- laughter poured/spewed from
- laughter ascended/floated up/ barreled up her throat
- ___ pulled/coaxed/thrust a laugh from him

Freed
(character giving in)
(can be applied to smiles)
- gave vent to her laughter
- gave way to mirth/rise to a laugh

- cut free a laugh
- allowed/permitted a rumbling chuckle
- let mirth fly free
- let amusement flush through
- let a laugh come full and free
- jettisoned/unpackaged/shed a ___ laugh
- embraced/welcomed a spate of laughter
- indulged/treated himself to a quiet chortle
- liberated/unleashed a laugh
- laugh he released felt good/tasted bitter coming out
- loosed a rash of mirth
- his laugh emerged ___

Restrained or Forced

- unshed laughter in her voice/statement (see also RESTRAINED [under SMILES AND LAUGHTER ONLY, pg. 165] in THESAURUS)
- laughing inside his mind
- laughter welled up inside
- snickered behind closed lips
- fended/fought off a laugh
- bit back a laugh

- rocked with silent laughter
- choked over contained laughter
- gagged on a laugh
- spare/greedy with her laughter
- affected/forced a laugh (see also FAKE [under SMILES AND LAUGHTER ONLY, pg. 164] in THESAURUS)

Failed

- couldn't find a laugh
- half-strangled/smothered laughter
- clipped off the end of his chortle
- laughter ran/petered out
- laughed, then let it run out
- cut her laughter short
- laughter cut out/faded/died
- his laugh ebbed/faltered
- silenced/muffled her laughter
- hid/concealed his amusement
- wound down to a hiccup
- checked his laughter
- laugh ended in a sputter

Negative Laughter

- laughter extinguished in a crackle of heat

- stifled a painful/pain-filled laugh
- laugh acquired a brittle edge/flavor
- turned curt
- a barbed laugh
- sawed out a bitter/humorless laugh
- a scoffing laugh
- laugh wasn't a good/happy sound
- laughed on an acidic splutter
- laughter lacked humor

> Laughter can be seen in other features, such as eyes crinkling and grooves etching around the mouth.

—FROWNS—

→ Substitutes for *frowned*: glowered, moped, pouted, sulked

Dissolving Smiles

His/her smile…
- fell into disrepair
- slipped/slid off his face
- flattened/collapsed

- twitched and died
- bled into a snarl
- melted/dripped off
- went rigid/stiff
- flipped to a frown
- ran out/fled her face
- withered/decayed/shriveled
- overturned/turned bitter
- didn't stick/stay long
- faded into
- ___ shadowed her smile
- smile lost/slipped its mooring

Sad Frowns

- something of sadness/heartbreak in her smile
- mouth sank into a sad smile
- lips curled out dejectedly
- lips twitching downward
- lips leveled with
- lower lip shot out
- lips stalwart/staunch with
- dropped her lower lip in a pout
- hurt/upset bent her lips down
- ___ worked a stiff frown onto his face
- grimace-smile/saggy smile/backward smile

- let her dismay show on her mouth
- frown lines creased/grooved the corner of his mouth
- frown etched into the side of his mouth
- a turned mouth
- frown hit/slammed him
- forehead turned frowny/grumpy
- mouth made an unimpressed/disgusted shape
- ___ carried his lips into a downturn
- plunged expression into a mope
- frown slashed/cut/forged across his face
- disappointment/misery weighted his lips
- frown line between her eyes
- an unhappy/crestfallen/dejected mouth
- a ___ (troubled/dismal) bent to his mouth
- frowned with his entire being/self/body
- narrowed a frown at
- full/shallow dip of a frown

Angry Frowns
- spread into a grim line
- mouth set at an unforgiving angle
- arranged her mouth in a sour/stern line
- glower breached his mouth
- bared/exposed her teeth
- a skull's sneer/grin
- mouth an intolerant slash
- lips thinned/narrowed
- trimmed lips to a harsh line
- a smile full of knives/needles
- presented a defiant/lip-curling snarl
- feral flash of teeth
- distorted smile
- a slash of a smile

Lips show sadness or displeasure by declining, dipping, drooping, sagging, sloping, slumping.

Chapter Thirteen: Jaw, Chin, and Throat

—JAW—

Hardening
- hard-set her jaw
- jaw slammed shut and hardened
- rigidity of his jaw
- cramp seized his tight jaw
- bulge in his jaw spasmed
- burning jaw
- jaw welded/locked shut
- carved out of ice/chiseled from steel/sculpted from iron
- jaw of iron/steel
- tight-jawed silence
- jaw-clenching madness/fury
- bitterness/anger grabbed him by the jaw
- muscle in his jaw bunched (see MUSCLE AND SINEW [pg. 31] for more)
- a muscle beat in his jaw
- ___ rippled the muscles of his jaw

- muscle feathered over his jaw
- jaw muscles firmed into a rigid line

Circling and Jutting

- worked his jaw in a tight circle
- jaw ruminated
- made deliberating circles
- jaw going/shifting/moving aslant
- jaw moved side to side (thinking)
- jaw protruded/jutted/thrust forward
- elongated her jaw
- sideways cock of the jaw
- stubborn bent to his jaw

Sagging

- jaw sagged/sank/dropped/fell open/slackened
- ___ parted/unhinged his jaw
- ___ slackened the tension in his jaw
- fell/snapped/hung/eked open
- ___ shocked his jaw lax
- shock unhitched his jaw
- hung suspended

- gape-jawed/slack-jawed/drop-jaw shock
- drifted open
- collected/recovered used of his jaw (closing jaw)

> -The jaw can tremble (wobble, clatter, etc.) with tears, anger or fear.
> -Jaw can be interchangeable with chin (see below).

—CHIN—

Up

- chin angled/jerked high
- chin at a proud tilt
- defiant/arrogant tilt to/lift of the chin
- cocked/lifted a degree
- heightened chin in challenge
- his chin went up
- a lofty chin
- superior lift of his chin
- boosted/hoisted her chin
- pitched high
- chin aimed high
- chin two ticks higher
- tipped chin steeply

- set chin to stubborn angle
- thrust out/up his chin
- notched up a few inches
- chin cut upward
- held his chin up
- wore her chin high
- wearing a high chin
- hiked a stubborn chin
- chin propped in the air
- chin reared up
- elevated/raised/upraised chin
- ___ drove chin upward

Down
- chin pulled in/ducked
- chin scraped his chest
- tucked/plunged/dipped her chin
- dropped chin to her chest
- chin drooped dejectedly
- a plummet of the chin
- chin took a nosedive
- chin settled low
- her lowered chin spoke words of ___ (surrender, etc.)
- chin slipped into submission
- ___ brought her chin in
- showed ___ in her descending chin

- couched/robed her lowered chin in
- chin positioned for ___ (deference, etc.)
- chin slumped with her shoulders

—THROAT and SWALLOWING—

-Substitutes for *throat*: airways, windpipe
-Structure of throat: cleft of his throat, column of her throat, cove/dip between the collar bones/clavicles, shallow/divot at the base of the throat

Tightening
- neck went taut
- lines of his throat tightened
- tendon in his neck twitched
- twisting sinews of her neck
- cord in his neck ticked/went hard
- cords of his neck began to protrude/were on prime display
- straining cords of the neck
- sinews stood out on his throat

Swallowing
- bulge of his throat wrenched up then down

- throat worked hard/wobbled
- throat lurched with a hard swallow
- the swell of his working throat
- Adam's apple bobbed/convulsed/jounced
- a gulp jerked her chin
- swallowed with a click
- forceful swallow worked his throat
- column of his throat rippled with a swallow
- swallowed to clear emotion/a knot
- planes of throat undulated with swallow
- swallowed past unshed tears/the squeeze of her throat
- through the strain of contained grief
- around the throbbing of her heart
- to make way for words
- lines of her neck moved as she swallowed

Dryness in Throat
- gulped through a dry patch/lump of words
- worked his throat through a sandy swallow
- dry patch resisted her swallow
- gulped through a dry throat
- throat screamed for moisture/water
- thirst-tortured throat
- throat dried from hastened/quickened breath
- parched throat
- ___ stripped her throat of moisture
- throat swollen with thirst
- ball of sawdust in his throat

See also TONGUE, WET/DRY (page 111).

Acid in Throat

→ Substitutes for *acid*: bile, bitterness, gorge, sour/biting/sharp/burning taste, or any intense emotion such as terror or fury

- acid sloshed a blistering trail up
- ___ spilled acid/bile up his throat
- acid rose/climbed
- gorge pushed up his throat
- bile slicked the back of throat
- thrust bile to the back of his mouth
- bile pooled at/leapt to the back of her throat
- churned his stomach up his throat
- scorched the length of his throat
- stomach tossed acid up
- sourness in the back of his throat

See also REBELLING in STOMACH AND CENTER (page 71).

Thickening or Aching

- ache moved down her throat
- ___ tore at her throat
- throat achingly thick
- ___ built in the back of her throat
- throat congested/plugged with emotion
- emotion welled in throat
- throat seized and knotted

- her throat a cinching belt
- cincture about her throat
- seemed a hand/fist/belt closed about her throat
- ___ enflamed his throat
- so thick it cut off breath/words
- throat ached with unshed tears
- sobs clogged her throat
- tears squeezed his throat
- centipedes/beetles crawled up and down his throat
- thick-as-sludge throat
- air whistled through constricted throat
- felt ___ like a sparrow/bee/sting in his throat
- ___ wrapped a hand around her throat
- fist about his windpipe
- ball of emotion clogged throat
- throat muscles straining to contain emotion
- throat closed up
- throat cramping painfully
- wheezed through the lump
- windpipe clamped
- ___ ballooned in his throat
- ___ gripped his throat

- a tormented throat
- throat developed an ache
- stone in his throat thickened
- lump formed deep in his throat
- anguish lodged in his throat
- stone pressed into her windpipe
- strangled the ___ in his throat
- back of her throat clicked audibly

Chapter Fourteen: Non-facial Emotion Beats

—EXPERIENCING EMOTION—

These eighty versatile beats can be used with just about any emotion, though the more intense ones (such as fear, anger, or passion) will find the best fit. The beats show the influence emotion has on the body as a whole or in part: bones, skin, muscles, soul, etc. These body parts are also widely interchangeable in these beats. Mix and match and watch your characters' emotions spring to life on the page.

- ___ pounded/drubbed/hammered her bones, nerves, or composure/resolve
- nerves sparked/snapped
- nerves stripped of their sheaths/stripped bare
- ___ titillated every nerve
- ___ inched along his skin
- ___ crushed her/his chest
- ___ stormed throughout his blood/veins/bones
- ___ cracked her rib-deep
- ___ rang deep in his bones

- ___ trundled through her
- ___ moved through/splintered his bones
- icy grasp/fingers around her stomach/spine/throat
- hot teeth of ___ bit into him/his backbone
- ___ seeped like rot through her bones
- ___ cracked bones from the inside out
- ___ rattled his bones
- shook him clear to his marrow
- bones felt hollow/brittle/cold with ___
- ___ splashed/drenched/dripped/poured/trickled through her/into her core/over her skin
- frame/body shook with ___
- ___ circled above him
- ___ seized his system
- ___ spiked him with adrenaline
- ___ sent him into despair/euphoria
- ___ lit up within him
- ___ coated her skin
- ___ hit/rode her hard
- ___ clawed to the surface
- gulped/gobbled down his ___

- sparked a filament of ___ inside
- a fine coat of ___ dusted him
- his bearing was ___
- doused her in ___
- ___ swathed him like a blanket
- thorny knot of emotion inside
- ripped strips from his heart/insides
- ___ shredded her heart
- a pin of ___ jabbed at ___
- ___ uncoiled his muscles
- every fiber/stitch of her felt ___
- ___ was aroused/kindled/provoked in her
- marshalled/rallied/collected his ___
- a shell/crust/skin of ___ around her
- ___ lapped at her
- ___ crept into her soul
- crust of his demeanor cracked/split/crumbled
- his ___ dried up/went dry
- ___ was broadcast all over her
- a cheer/warning trumpeted through
- ___ shot through him
- ___-riddled body/soul

153

- a suspect/suspicious show of ___
- every curve/line of her body spoke ___
- sparks of ___ flickered around his brain
- ___ in the air wrenched/whipped/lashed at her
- her pain/happiness strummed/buzzed/hummed into him
- ___ enwrapped/encased/shrouded his spine
- ___ snaking/twining/threading around him hard
- felt a splinter/shard of ___
- enshrouded herself in ___
- ___ shuddered/shimmied through her
- lustering with ___
- ___ singed her composure
- she showed him her ___ (fear, defiance, etc.)
- an air of ___ cloaked her
- ___ colored him/tinted his eyes
- ___ stirred within him
- sluiced him with waves of ___
- his ___ flared
- ___ drew her painfully inward
- body was shredded/frazzled/

- tattered/worn thin with ___
- body pulled in on itself
- ___ frayed him
- something ___ sank through her
- fashioned himself like flint
- squall whipped up within her
- storm swept over him/across her features
- restless/angry energy prowled inside
- ___ slithered/snaked/coiled through him
- felt her ___ swell/dwindle
- gave a full measure of ___
- ___ swarmed her/crested over her/took possession of her
- ___ scoured/scored him with raking claws/talons
- ___ girded/clothed/shrouded him
- heart/soul rich with ___
- ___ prevailed upon him
- ___ charged in for an assault/attack/blindside

—CONTAINING or FALSIFYING EMOTION—

- retracted a well of ___
- ___ clamped her heart
- thick with false sorrow
- demeanor remained guarded/impassive
- sucked in his cheeks
- kicked down her fear
- denied ___ that rose in him
- dampened the ___ within
- numbness consumed her
- body felt leaden
- affected a pose of ___

Chapter Fifteen: Thesaurus

One of the challenges an author faces is creating original content, but sometimes, a passage calls for simplicity, for tried-and-true. That's where this thesaurus comes in.

It's only a drop of the great sea of synonyms and certainly not meant as a be-all and end-all. Instead, consider it simply as a ready supply of adjectives frequently used in fiction to describe *expressions*, *gazes*, *smiles*, and *laughter*.

Use the thesaurus to fill any blank in the beats provided in this book, but don't limit yourself to these. When you come up with your own, add them here. Space has been left between each entry for that purpose.

The adjectives have been divided into categories based on which of the four beats listed above they can be best applied to. Some cannot be used interchangeably but many can.

—EXPRESSIONS, GAZES, SMILES—

Amiable: affable, benevolent, friendly, genial, gentle, innocuous, kind, loving, peaceful, pleasant, serene, soft-as-___ (satin, seed fluff, silk, etc.), tender, warm

_____
_____
_____
_____
_____
_____

Angry: acute, bloodless, brittle, bullish, cross, fiery/with fire, flinty, forceful, glowering, hard, implacable, irascible, liquid-fire, livid, mad, petulant, pinched, prickly, put-upon, raging, rigid, salty, scathing, severe, sore, strident, tart, tight-lipped, thin, toxic, truculent, turned, uncaged, winter, turbulent

___
___
___
___

Arrogant: austere, censorious, cocky, contemptuous, degrading, disdainful, haughty, high-handed, imperious, of hauteur, pompous, superior, unctuous

___
___
___
___

Bitter: acidic, astringent, caustic, disaffected, grudging, harsh, jealous, mordant, rancorous, resentful, scornful, unsweetened, tart, vinegary, virulent

___
___
___
___

Bright: beaming, brilliant, burnished, cheery, cloudless, glimmering, glowing, gossamer, illuminating, luminous, radiant, shining, sparkling, sunny, twinkling

___

Challenging: audacious, bold, daring, defiant, forbidding, game, impudent, questioning, provoking, testing

Confused: addled, befuddled, bemused, bewildered, dazed, hazy, lost, muddy, mystified, perplexed, puzzled, stupefied.

Crafty: arch, canny, cunning, disingenuous, fraudulent, scheming, shrewd, slick, sneaky, sly, snide, tricky, wily

Cryptic: ambiguous, coded, dark, doubting, evasive, furtive, hidden, knowing, murky, mysterious, secret, secret-filled, vague

Disgusted: afflicted, appalled, loathing, nauseated, offended, repulsed, revolted, scandalized, shocked, sickened

Flat: barren, benign, blank-, empty-, or dead-eyed, bland, blasé, detached, drab, emotionless, hollow, humorless, shuttered, vapid
  Laughter only: colorless, monotone, toneless

Flirtatious: amorous, artful, coquettish, come-hither, coy, dallying, flirty, philandering, provocative, saucy, teasing, vixen

Happy: amused, cheery, courteous, dancing, encouraging, genial, gleeful, good-humored, jocose, jocular, jolly, jovial, joyous, plucked/plucky, sanguine, triumphant, vivacious
  Laughter only: bubbly, effervescent

Infectious: bewitching, captivating, catching, compelling, dazzling, disarming, enchanting, enrapturing, irresistible, magnetic

Lazy: careless, dawdling, idle, indolent, lackadaisical, leisurely, lethargic, placid, relaxed, shiftless, sleepy, sluggish, slumberous, torpid, truant

Sad: barren, bleak, brooding, cheerless, dejected, dimmed, dismayed, dour, dreary, gaunt, gloomy, joyless, melancholy, mournful, pained, pain-filled, pitiful, sorrowful, tragic, tristful, weepy, wrecked, wretched

Sarcastic: cutting, cynical, droll, dry, ironic, jaded, mocking, mordant, sardonic, scornful, snide, taunting

___
___
___
___

Sensual: bawdy, carnal, erotic, heady, iniquitous, febrile, feverish, fiery/with fire, foxy, lewd, lusty, mesmerizing, of pleasure, sensuous, sexual, sexy, silky, sinful, sultry, steamy, vulgar
  <u>Smiles only</u>: buttery, devastating, dizzying

___
___
___
___

Stately: courtly, dignified, elegant, enigmatic, graceful, gracious, imperial, kingly, queenly, lofty, lordly, majestic, polite, proper, urbane

___
___
___
___

Guarded: careful, cautious, disaffected, distancing, skeptical, leery, reserved, unattached, suspicious, tentative, wary
  <u>Smiles only</u>—closed-mouth/lipped, drawn

___
___

Unbelieving: astonished, astounded, denying, disbelieving, doubting, edgy, fearful, incredulous, jarred, rejecting, shocked

Wicked: black, cruel, dangerous, dark, deadly, devilish, devious, feral, festering, filthy, hard-as-___ (hate, stone, etc.), hellacious, inky, lecherous, malignant, murderous, nasty, pointed, roguish, satanic, savage, sinister, sneering, soulless, stormy, waspish, vicious, vile, violent, wolfish

—SMILES and LAUGHTER ONLY—

Crazed: demented, deranged, feral, hysterical, maddened, manic, psycho, savage, unbalanced, unrestrained, wild

---

Fake: artful, artificial, bogus, contrived, counterfeit, farce/farcical, faux, forged, obliging, plastic, propped-up, required, staged, stiff, wooden

---

Inadvertent: accidental, heedless, sneaky, unconscious, unintended, unintentional, unmindful, unthinking, unwitting

---

Playful: blithesome, breezy, carefree, chummy, comic, easy, impish, puckish, sublime, waggish, whimsical, winning, winsome

---

Relaxed: casual, creeping, gradual, light, measured, nascent, reluctant, slow, slow-building, unhurried

Restrained: bottled, bridled, choked back, held back, jailed, kept down, killed, repressed, unshed, restrained, withheld

Shaky: broken, feeble, flimsy, fragile, halfhearted, nervous, rickety, shy, sickly, stuttering, timorous, wobbly, worried

Short: barked, clipped, crisp, curt, fleeting, infinitesimal, perfunctory, pithy, stilted, stunted, tense, terse, tight, trifle

Youthful: boyish, chipper, coltish, frisky, frolicsome/ frolicking, girlish, jaunty, lively, rollicking, sprightly, spry

—EXPRESSIONS and GAZES ONLY—

Cutting: barbed, brittle, frigid, frosty, gimlet, hateful, intolerant, quelling, nasty, severe, snappish/snapping, stony, withering

---

Direct: blunt, candid, clear, even, frank, honest, lineal, meaningful, naked, open, pointed, straight

---

Emotionless: aloof, blank, cold, cool, dead-eyed, deadpan, detached, distant, drugged, dry, empty, faraway, foggy, glazed, hazy/hazily, impassive, muddied, poker-faced, remote, stolid, stared through, unspeaking, unmoved, withdrawn

---

Evasive: cagey, cursory, shifty, slippery

Insolent: churlish, cogent, mulish, stubborn, taciturn

Long/Fixed: abiding, constant, drawn-out, even, inflexible, immutable, immovable, implacable, lengthy, lingering, protracted, relentless, stable, steady, unrelenting, unyielding

Reading: calculating, introspective, questioning, quizzical, scouring, speculative, thinking

Sad: baleful, bottomless, fervid, glassy, haunted, pain-soaked, soulful (see also TEARS [pg. 100])

Sensual: caressing, concupiscent, greedy, heated, hungry, lustful, naked, racy, smoky, smoldering, will-shattering

Wicked: blistering, drumming, hammering, inclement, sizzling

—SMILES ONLY—

Beautiful: alluring, dazzling, ethereal, exquisite, lovely, otherworldly, resplendent, stunning, sublime, supernal, wonderous

---

Huge: beatific, blue-ribbon, bright, broad, capitol, cracking, divine, fat, generous, giant, gilt-edged, magnificent, plentiful, prizewinning, quality, sterling, toothy, unabridged

---

Small: dim, faint, mellow, pinched, scrawny, shallow, understated, tight-lipped, trifle, wan

---

Sprite: fay, imp, pixie, siren, sylph

—LAUGHTER ONLY—

Breathy: airy, breathless, blown, short-winded

Full: boisterous, booming, deep-barreled, deep-chest, free, full-blown, hardy, healthy, hearty, liberal, ribald, rich, robust, rumbling, peppy, strapping, trumpeting, unending, unfettered, uproarious

Musical: arioso, belling, gliding, golden, harp-like, quicksilver, marching, melodious, ringing, silvery/silvern, singing/singsong, spirited/with spirit, tinkling, trilling, up-tempo

Piercing: cackling, gimlet, grating, sharp, shrieking, shrill, strident

Quiet: low, low-pitched, muted, reserved, reticent, thin

Bonus Material: Dialogue Tags

What is a tag?

A dialogue tag attributes a line of dialogue to a character. They also show volume, tone, and emotion. They should be used as sparingly as possible. (A quick Google search or quality craft book will educate you more fully on tags and their proper uses.)

Tag. You're it?

You'll find there's a debate on the use of tags, whether to stick to the basics (*said* and *asked*) or broaden the horizon to any number of tags. *Said* and *asked* are rarely bad choices, and they're easy for readers to ignore, allowing them focus to remain on the dialogue. However, limiting the use of any tag besides those two has potential to stunt an author's voice. It can also make for a colder, more mechanical style—not a bad thing for certain genres (sci-fi or dystopian, to name two), but it's not an all-purpose tone.

Even those who preach against tag restriction won't argue that the below tags are *telling*. (Show versus tell—another important lesson in craft you shouldn't miss!) While *telling* does have its place in fiction, any author or editor who knows their stuff will strongly encourage *showing*. Enter the 2,500 templates in this book.

Overuse of *telling* is lazy writing, as is overuse of tags. It's also a clear indicator of an amateur—something no author wants when submitting to an agent. To avoid this, before reaching for a tag, try an action beat that informs the reader who is speaking, and always create the strongest dialogue possible—dialogue that *shows* bickering, for example, instead of ending dialogue by *telling* the reader, "she bickered."

Tag me.

There's no getting around certain instances where a telling tag is necessary. They can speed up a lagging scene by removing the wordier use of an action beat. Doing this also keeps word count down because *showing* is almost always wordier than *telling*. Another important use is adding color through vocal nuance, such as volume or tonal quality. After all, the only way for a reader to know the male lead is whispering is to *tell* her, "he whispered."

The following list is also useful for inspiration on the narrative front when your brain is on the fritz or for filling in the blanks in our handy-dandy templates. Many of the words can also be repurposed for tone of voice.

Anger/Clipped Speech
accused
admonished
argued
badgered
bickered
bit out/back
challenged
charged
chided
clipped
complained
corrected
countered
cursed
dared
demanded
demurred
disagreed
fired off

goaded
grudged
huffed
insulted
jeered
jibed
mocked
muttered
objected
pestered
provoked
quipped
refused
rejected
retaliated
retorted
sassed
scoffed
scolded
seethed
snapped
snarled
snipped
spat/spat out
swore
taunted
threatened
threw out
warned
withered

Happiness/Laughing
beamed
bubbled
cackled
cheeped
cheered
chimed
chirped
chirruped
chortled
chorused
chuckled
clucked
complimented
congratulated
cooed
crooned
drawled
effused
encouraged
exulted
giggled
gurgled
gushed
hummed
intoned
jested
joked
laughed
praised

purred
sang
simpered
teased
thanked
trilled
twittered

Sadness/Crying
apologized
babbled
bawled
blubbered
brooded
comforted
consoled
cried
lamented
mumbled
pleaded
sighed
sniffed
sniffled
sobbed
spilled
wailed
wept
worried

Fear/Broken Speech
begged
choked
coughed up
croaked
denied
doubted
dribbled
eked out
fretted
garbled
gasped out
gibbered
got out
groaned
gulped
implored
lisped
moaned
panted
pleaded
pled
prayed
quavered
rattled
slurred
spluttered
sputtered
squeaked
squealed

stammered
stuttered
wheezed
whimpered
whined
whispered
worried

Stating/Explaining
addressed
articulated
chimed in
clarified
commented
contributed
conveyed
delivered
described
explained
expressed
gave words to
informed
instructed
mentioned
noted
notified
observed
offered
opined
pointed out
related
remarked
reported
sounded
spoke
stated
testified
told
vocalized
voiced

Replying
answered
came back at
came back with
pinged back
rejoined
replied
responded
returned

Questioning/Wondering
asked
considered
inquired
mused
pondered
queried
questioned
quizzed

requested
wondered

Adding/Interrupting
added
broke in
cut in
interjected
jumped in
piled on
put forth
put in
volunteered

Continuing/Repeating
blathered
chatted
chattered
continued
declaimed
droned
echoed
gabbered
imitated
jabbered
lectured
mimicked
prattled
quoted
repeated
restated
resumed
went on
yakked
yapped

Proclaiming/Promising
aired
announced
avowed
claimed
declared
piped
proclaimed
promised
pronounced
vowed

Agreeing
acknowledged
acquiesced
admitted
affirmed
afforded
agreed
allowed
approved
came out with
conceded

Deceiving/Evasion
balked
concocted
deflected
dissembled
evaded
exaggerated
fibbed
lied
waffled

Guessing/Using Caution
cautioned
conjectured
guessed
hazarded
hypothesized
reasoned
speculated
surmised
tested
theorized
ventured

Suggesting/Using Discretion
confided
hinted
implied
intimated
proposed
suggested

Pushing One's Opinion
advised
asserted
bugged
cajoled
coached
coaxed
commanded
convinced
defended
insisted
nagged
ordered
pressed
protested
pushed
reiterated
stressed
urged

Deciding/Reassuring
assured
concluded
confirmed
decided
held

held to
maintained
reassured

Surprise
bleated
blurted
burst out
coughed out
exclaimed
gasped out
marveled
perplexed
puzzled
yelped

Bragging
blustered
boasted
bragged
crowed
gloated
spouted
swaggered

Remembering
called up
cited
conjured
recalled
recollected
recounted
relived
remembered
reminded
reminisced
summoned
summoned up
thought back

Revealing
blabbed
broadcast
confessed
disclosed
divulged
gave away
leaked
let slip
made known
owned up
revealed
spilled
tipped off
uncovered

Consoling
appeased
assuaged
calmed

hushed
mollified
smoothed over
softened
soothed
sympathized

Stopping/Starting
began
broke off
clipped off
cut short
dismissed
drove ahead
ended
finished
greeted
launched into
stalled
started
welcomed
wrapped up

Growling/Grumbling
grated
graveled
graveled out
grit/gritted out
ground out
growled
grumbled
grunted out
rumbled
scratched out

Voice Raised
barked
bellowed
boomed
called
called out
exploded
flared
hailed
hollered
howled
raged
ranted
resounded
roared
screamed
screeched
shot/shot back
shouted
shrieked
shrilled
stormed
thundered
yelled

Voice Lowered
aired/airy voice
breathed
hissed
hummed
mouthed
mumbled
muttered
rasped out
susurrated/susurrus
wheezed

Whisper Beats
- a throat/voice-roughening whisper
- asked on a hush
- expelled words on a ___ whisper
- current of a breath carried his words
- cut her voice low/her volume off at the knees
- dulled/dulled by/dulled down to a whisper
- falling/descending volume
- hushed timbre tight with ___
- in intimate tones
- lisping half under the breath
- lowered volume/tone/voice
- muted tone, timbre, etc.
- on brusque hiss
- pitched his voice low/quiet
- power-whisper
- raspy/secretive hush
- said in a hum/a murmur
- said in an undertone
- said on a sibilant hiss
- said on a wisp/a rough sigh/a whispery breath/a low thrum
- scant/breathy/wispy volume
- severed his volume to (just above) a whisper
- she hushed the word
- speaking in a (mock) hush
- spoke lowly
- spoke sotto voce
- subdued/muffled/faint inflection
- subdued/tamed tone

- suffocated voice
- thin/bare/soft/gentle voice
- turned his volume down
- under his breath
- uttered for her alone/his ears only/just them two
- uttered/murmured on a breath
- voice a feather's brush/a whisper of wind/a slight caress
- voice a mere tiptoe
- voice a semblance of the wind
- voice a shred of a whisper
- voice barely overrode
- voice drifting on a/floating on a whisper
- voice faded into a wisp
- voice fallen
- voice half-gentle/half-strong/half-volume
- voice quietening/shrinking/dwindling/gentling
- voice riding/traveling a whisper
- voice so quiet it sounded as though lost in a gale
- voice sounding far away
- volume wanting/skimpy/slight/insubstantial/slender
- whispered around the ___ in her throat
- whispered in a rough texture
- whisper-shouted
- words a mere push of air

Author Bio:

APRIL W GARDNER is an award-winning author who proudly waves an indie flag. Her great passion is historical romance with themes of Native American and Southeastern U.S. culture. Copyeditor, late-bloomer college kid, and mother of two, she lives in South Texas. In no particular order, April dreams of owning a horse, learning a third language, and visiting all the national parks.

Connect with April online at:

Facebook:
www.facebook.com/april.gardner1/

Website:
www.aprilgardner.com

Email:
aprilgardnerwrites@gmail.com

Made in the USA
Las Vegas, NV
10 October 2021